"Set a guard over my mouth Lord. Keep watch... lips."

Lord Jesu[s]... with all...

To you Lord... your... goodness. Please come & make-up what is lacking in my efforts. Lord I trust in you."

May God banish all anxiety of from our midst. Heal all our ills & fill... our hearts... with... peace... through... Christ our life come...

Lord Jesu[s] come & stay with me. Fill my life with your peace, my home with your presence & my heart with your praise! Help me to show kindness, mercy & goodness to all even to those who cause me ill will or harm.

CATHOLIC
MASS & PRAYER JOURNAL

Photography by Julie Durr
Copyright © 2016 Julie Durr

ISBN-13: 978-1534816121
ISBN-10: 1534816127

ISBN-13: 978-1534816121
ISBN-10: 1534816127

Dedication

I dedicate this journal to all those like me, who seek to know God. I also dedicate this journal to those who have inspired me by how they live their Catholic faith and show the love of God through their actions, thoughts and words. Thank you.

Books of the Old Testament and Abbreviations

Genesis- Gen	Exodus- Ex	Leviticus-Lev	Numbers-Num
Deuteronomy-Deut	Joshua-Josh	Judges-Judg	Ruth-Ruth
1Samuel-1Sam	2Samuel-2Sam	1Kings-1Kings	2Kings-2Kings
1Chronicles-1Chr	2Chronicles-2Chr	Ezra-Ezra	Nehemiah-Neh
Tobit-Tob	Judith-Jdt	Esther-Esth	1Maccabees-1Macc
2Maccabees-2Macc	Job-Job	Psalms-Ps	Proverbs-Prov
Ecclesiates-Eccl	Song of Solomon-Songs	Canticles-Cant	Wisdom-Wis
Sirach-Sir	Isaiah-Isa	Jeremiah-Jer	Lamentations-Lam
Baruch-Bar	Ezekial-Ezek	Daniel-Dan	Hosea-Hos
Joel-Joel	Amos-Am	Jonah-Jon	Micah-Mic
Nahum-Nah	Habakkuk-Hab	Zephaniah-Zeph	
Haggai-Hag	Zechariah-Zech	Malachi-Mal	

Books of the New Testament and Abbreviations

Matthew-Mt	Mark-Mk	Luke-Lk	John -Jn
Acts of Apostles-Acts	Romans-Rom	1Corinthians-1Cor	2Corinthians-2Cor
Galatians-Gal	Ephesians-Eph	Philippians-Phil	Colossians-Col
1Thessalonians-1Thess	2Thessalonians-2Thess	1Timothy-1Tim	2Timothy-2Tim
Titus-Titus	Philemon-Phil	Hebrews-Heb	James-James
1Peter-1Pet	2Peter-2Pet	1John-1Jn	2John-2Jn
3John-3Jn	Jude-Jude	Revelation-Rev	Apocalypse-Apoc

The Order of the Mass

Introductory Rites:

Entrance:

Penitential Act:

Gloria:

Opening Prayer:

Liturgy of the Week:

Scripture Readings:

Homily:

Profession of Faith:

General Intercessions:

The Collection:

Liturgy of the Eucharist:

The Offeratory:

Eucharistic Prayer:

The Consecration:

The Lord's Prayer:

Sign of Peace:

Communion:

Thanksgiving:

Concluding Rites:

Final Blessing:

Dismissal:

Apostle's Creed

I believe in God, the Father Almighty,
Creator of heaven and earth;
and in Jesus Christ, His only Son, our Lord:
Who was conceived by the Holy Spirit,
born of the Virgin Mary;
suffered under Pontius Pilate,
was crucified,
died
and was buried.

He descended into hell;
the third day He rose again from the dead;
He ascended into heaven,
is seated at the right hand of God the Father
Almighty;
from thence He shall come to judge
the living and the dead.

I believe in the Holy Spirit, the Holy Catholic
Church, the communion of Saints, the forgive-
ness of sins, the resurrection of the body, and
life everlasting.

Amen.

In the name of the Father,

and of the Son,

and of the Holy Spirit.

Amen.

"For me, prayer is a surge of the heart; it is a simple look turned towards heaven; it is a cry of recognition and love; embracing both trial and joy."
– Saint Therese of Lisieux, *Story of a Soul*

January 1

Reflections: Mass, Homily & Scriptures

Date:

	Book	Chapter	Verses
1st Reading			
Responsorial			
2nd Reading			
Verse			
Gospel			

Notes

Restore me dear Notes ord restore me
Fr I know you hear me
you always hear me. God
I release my concerns to you
as I write them down. Thank
you for loving me so much
that you are concerned with
each entry no matter how
great or small. Fr help me
to hold unto my peace today no
matter what comes my way.
Mother Mary hold my hand
you will you can make me ?

✝ Reflections ✝

Jesus I Trusted you
Mary kept all these
things in her heart. Jesus
a new year, new challenge,
new happenings. My Savior,
Mother Mary help me to
look to you for strength
courage & wisdom for this
new year.

I pray for so many today.
Joani my sweet Jes Chris
Gary Sal. Mick & myself
Mary Lou & all my family
I pray for peace for our
Country & peace on this
beautiful earth you have given
us.

Thank You Lord

Thank you Lord for all the
love, mercy, forgiveness to me
this day & always. Please
I give you. My Jesus keep
me to just peace in my heart.
Thank you for life!

Daily Reflections

My Jesus, I believe that You are present in the Most Holy Sacrament. I love You above all things, and I desire to receive You into my soul. Since I cannot at this moment receive You sacramentally, come at least spiritually into my heart. I embrace You as if You were already there and unite myself wholly to You. Never permit me to be separated from You. Amen.

Sunday		
Monday		
Tuesday		
Wednesday		
Thursday		
Friday		
Saturday		

The Spiritual Works of Mercy

To admonish sinners
To instruct the ignorant
To counsel the doubtful
To comfort the sorrowful
To bear wrongs patiently
To forgive all injuries
To pray for the living and the dead

I T r u s t J e s u s

The Corporal Works of Mercy

To feed the hungry
To give drink to the thirsty
To clothe the naked
To visit and ransom the captives
To shelter the homeless
To visit the sick
To bury the dead

Prayers & Answers

Date: 1/1/19	Date:
Prayer: _Healing for Juani_ _Good results for Jen_	Prayer:
Answer:	Answer:

Daily Examination of Conscience

Sins:	Pride	Greed	Gluttony	Lust	Sloth	Envy	Anger
Virtues:	Humily	Generosity	Abstinence	Chastity	Diligence	Kindness	Patience

Sunday		
Monday		*Help me to get rid of anger*
Tuesday		*Help me show more kindness*
Wednesday		
Thursday		
Friday		
Saturday		

Act of Contrition

M
e
r
c
y

My God, I am sorry for my sins with all my heart. In
choosing to do wrong and failing to do good, I have
sinned against you whom I should love above all
things. I firmly intend, with your help, to do penance,
to sin no more, and to avoid whatever leads me to
sin. Our Savior Jesus Christ suffered and died for us.
In His name, my God, have mercy on us.

F
o
r
g
i
v
e
n
e
s
s

Amen.

Prayers & Answers

Date:	Date:
Prayer:	Prayer:
Answer:	Answer:

Reflections: Mass, Homily & Scriptures

Date: 1/2/19

	Book	Chapter	Verses
1st Reading			
Responsorial			
2nd Reading			
Verse			
Gospel			

Notes

Before me today as I begin. Restore me
To thank you for hearing me
& know you always hear me
God I release my concerns to you
as I write them down. Thank you
for loving me so much that you
are concerned with each
entry no matter how great or small
Mother May pull my heart
To help me to hold fast my resolve
today no matter what comes my way
& You will you can make me clear
Jesus I trust in you

✞ Reflections ✞

My Lord a new year. New
beginnings. Lord help me
to stay close to you this
Year. There are some
challenging days ahead.
I pray for my Jen to love
the strangers. I pray
for you my Lord to stay
by her side. I pray
all will be well

Thank You Lord

Thank you Lord for this
day. Thank you for this
time with you - For being
able to rest. For warmth
I pray for all those who
are homeless. Please find
shelter for them.

Daily Reflections

My Jesus, I believe that You are present in the Most Holy Sacrament. I love You above all things, and I desire to receive You into my soul. Since I cannot at this moment receive You sacramentally, come at least spiritually into my heart. I embrace You as if You were already there and unite myself wholly to You. Never permit me to be separated from You. Amen.

Sunday		
Monday		
Tuesday		
Wednesday		
Thursday		
Friday		
Saturday		

The Spiritual Works of Mercy

To admonish sinners
To instruct the ignorant
To counsel the doubtful
To comfort the sorrowful
To bear wrongs patiently
To forgive all injuries
To pray for the living and the dead

The Corporal Works of Mercy

To feed the hungry
To give drink to the thirsty
To clothe the naked
To visit and ransom the captives
To shelter the homeless
To visit the sick
To bury the dead

Prayers & Answers

Date: 1/2/19	Date:
Prayer: *[handwritten]*	Prayer:
Answer:	Answer:

Daily Examination of Conscience

Sins:	Pride	Greed	Gluttony	Lust	Sloth	Envy	Anger
Virtues:	Humily	Generosity	Abstinence	Chastity	Diligence	Kindness	Patience

Sunday		
Monday		
Tuesday		
Wednesday		
Thursday		
Friday		
Saturday		

Act of Contrition

M
e
r
c
y

My God, I am sorry for my sins with all my heart. In
choosing to do wrong and failing to do good, I have
sinned against you whom I should love above all
things. I firmly intend, with your help, to do penance,
to sin no more, and to avoid whatever leads me to
sin. Our Savior Jesus Christ suffered and died for us.
In His name, my God, have mercy on us.

F
o
r
g
i
v
e
n
e
s
s

Amen.

Prayers & Answers

Date:	Date:
Prayer:	Prayer:
Answer:	Answer:

Reflections: Mass, Homily & Scriptures

Date: 1/3/19

	Book	Chapter	Verses
1st Reading			
Responsorial			
2nd Reading			
Verse			
Gospel			

Notes

To thank you for hearing me
I know you always heal me
God I release my concerns to
you as I write them down.
Thank you for loving me so much
that you are concerned with
everything no matter how great or
small. Restore me Jesus one
Restore me to help me to pull out
my plan today no matter what comes
my way. Mother Mary lead me to your Son
If you will you can make me clean
Jesus I trust ✝ in you.

✝ Reflections ✝

Holy Spirit come into my
heart. Help me to see
Jesus around me. Help
me to be grateful. It is
1:53 Thursday am. Jesus help
me to sleep so I can be
refreshed to do your will
for me. I pray to my Jesus
& for Joseph God

Thank You Lord

For this time with you
even at 1:53 Am. Thank
you for life + the people in
my life & help me to stay
positive about my Jen

Daily Reflections

My Jesus, I believe that You are present in the Most Holy Sacrament. I love You above all things, and I desire to receive You into my soul. Since I cannot at this moment receive You sacramentally, come at least spiritually into my heart. I embrace You as if You were already there and unite myself wholly to You. Never permit me to be separated from You. Amen.

Sunday		
Monday		
Tuesday		
Wednesday		
Thursday		
Friday		
Saturday		

The Spiritual Works of Mercy

To admonish sinners

To instruct the ignorant

To counsel the doubtful

To comfort the sorrowful

To bear wrongs patiently

To forgive all injuries

To pray for the living and the dead

I T r u s t

J e s u s

The Corporal Works of Mercy

To feed the hungry

To give drink to the thirsty

To clothe the naked

To visit and ransom the captives

To shelter the homeless

To visit the sick

To bury the dead

Prayers & Answers

Date:	Date:
Prayer:	Prayer:
Answer:	Answer:

Daily Examination of Conscience

Sins:	Pride	Greed	Gluttony	Lust	Sloth	Envy	Anger
Virtues:	Humily	Generosity	Abstinence	Chastity	Diligence	Kindness	Patience

Sunday		
Monday		
Tuesday		
Wednesday		
Thursday		
Friday		
Saturday		

Act of Contrition

M
e
r
c
y

My God, I am sorry for my sins with all my heart. In
choosing to do wrong and failing to do good, I have
sinned against you whom I should love above all
things. I firmly intend, with your help, to do penance,
to sin no more, and to avoid whatever leads me to
sin. Our Savior Jesus Christ suffered and died for us.
In His name, my God, have mercy on us.

F
o
r
g
i
v
e
n
e
s
s

Amen.

Prayers & Answers

Date:	Date:
Prayer:	Prayer:
Answer:	Answer:

Reflections: Mass, Homily & Scriptures

Date: 1/4/19

	Book	Chapter	Verses
1st Reading			
Responsorial			
2nd Reading			
Verse			
Gospel			

Notes

To thank you for hearing me
I know you always hear me
God I release my concerns
to you as I write them down.
Thank you for loving me so
much that you are concerned
with each entry no matter
how great or small Restore me
Settle soul restore me to help me
to live onto my peace today no
matter what comes my way. I ☩ you
will you can make me clear. Thank
you God ☩ **Reflections** ☩ Jesus I ask for

My Jesus help me to be
a truly sign greater of God
Some in life & struggles
compel us — me to be
resentful & angry. There is
no purpose in this. There is
no joy in this. Help me
each day to be ever so
thankful. Praise & honor
my Jesus. Help me to live

my life in your presence".

Thank You Lord

Thank You Lord for life.
Thank You Lord for love.
Thank You Lord for friendship.
Thank You Lord!

Daily Reflections

My Jesus, I believe that You are present in the Most Holy Sacrament. I love You above all things, and I desire to receive You into my soul. Since I cannot at this moment receive You sacramentally, come at least spiritually into my heart. I embrace You as if You were already there and unite myself wholly to You. Never permit me to be separated from You. Amen.

Sunday		
Monday		
Tuesday		
Wednesday		
Thursday		
Friday		
Saturday		

The Spiritual Works of Mercy	I T r u s t	The Corporal Works of Mercy
To admonish sinners		To feed the hungry
To instruct the ignorant		To give drink to the thirsty
To counsel the doubtful		To clothe the naked
To comfort the sorrowful	J e s u s	To visit and ransom the captives
To bear wrongs patiently		To shelter the homeless
To forgive all injuries		To visit the sick
To pray for the living and the dead		To bury the dead

Prayers & Answers

Date:	Date:
Prayer:	Prayer:
Answer:	Answer:

Daily Examination of Conscience

Sins:	Pride	Greed	Gluttony	Lust	Sloth	Envy	Anger
Virtues:	Humily	Generosity	Abstinence	Chastity	Diligence	Kindness	Patience

Sunday		
Monday		
Tuesday		
Wednesday		
Thursday		
Friday		
Saturday		

Act of Contrition

M
e
r
c
y

My God, I am sorry for my sins with all my heart. In choosing to do wrong and failing to do good, I have sinned against you whom I should love above all things. I firmly intend, with your help, to do penance, to sin no more, and to avoid whatever leads me to sin. Our Savior Jesus Christ suffered and died for us. In His name, my God, have mercy on us.

Forgivencess

Amen.

Prayers & Answers

Date:	Date:
Prayer:	Prayer:
Answer:	Answer:

Reflections: Mass, Homily & Scriptures

Date: 1/5/19

	Book	Chapter	Verses
1st Reading			
Responsorial			
2nd Reading			
Verse			
Gospel			

Notes

Fr thank you for hearing me
I know you always hear me. God
I release my concerns to you as
I write them down. Thank you
for loving me so much that you
are concerned with each entry
no matter how great or small -
Restore me heal me Fr restore me. Fr help
me to hold onto my peace today no matter
what comes my way. May lead to you for
you will you don me Jen dear
Jesus I trust in you

✝ Reflections ✝

My Jesus thank you for
always hearing me. My Savior
I am distracted a little these
day. I should not worry,
I need to trust you will bring
good out of this situation
with my sweet soul. I pray
Jesus for strength + faith Fr
I know you will Fr the care
Jen ✝

Thank You Lord

Thank you for life!
Thank you for my sight being
able to read your beautiful
word.
Thank you for friends —

Daily Reflections

My Jesus, I believe that You are present in the Most Holy Sacrament. I love You above all things, and I desire to receive You into my soul. Since I cannot at this moment receive You sacramentally, come at least spiritually into my heart. I embrace You as if You were already there and unite myself wholly to You. Never permit me to be separated from You. Amen.

Sunday		
Monday		
Tuesday		
Wednesday		
Thursday		
Friday		
Saturday		

The Spiritual Works of Mercy

To admonish sinners
To instruct the ignorant
To counsel the doubtful
To comfort the sorrowful
To bear wrongs patiently
To forgive all injuries
To pray for the living and the dead

Treasures

The Corporal Works of Mercy

To feed the hungry
To give drink to the thirsty
To clothe the naked
To visit and ransom the captives
To shelter the homeless
To visit the sick
To bury the dead

Prayers & Answers

Date:	Date:
Prayer:	Prayer:
Answer:	Answer:

Daily Examination of Conscience

Sins:	Pride	Greed	Gluttony	Lust	Sloth	Envy	Anger
Virtues:	Humily	Generosity	Abstinence	Chastity	Diligence	Kindness	Patience

Sunday		
Monday		
Tuesday		
Wednesday		
Thursday		
Friday		
Saturday		

Act of Contrition

M
e
r
c
y

My God, I am sorry for my sins with all my heart. In choosing to do wrong and failing to do good, I have sinned against you whom I should love above all things. I firmly intend, with your help, to do penance, to sin no more, and to avoid whatever leads me to sin. Our Savior Jesus Christ suffered and died for us. In His name, my God, have mercy on us.

F
o
r
g
i
v
e
n
e
s
s

Amen.

Prayers & Answers

Date:	Date:
Prayer:	Prayer:
Answer:	Answer:

Grace to you and peace
from God…

Glory to God in the
Highest

Our Father

Our Father, Who art in Heaven,
Hallowed be Thy Name.

Thy Kingdom come.
Thy will be done, on earth
as it is in Heaven.
Give us this day our daily bread.

And forgive us our trespasses, as we forgive
those who trespass against us.

And lead us not into temptation,
but deliver us from evil.

Amen.

Reflections: Mass, Homily & Scriptures

Date:

	Book	Chapter	Verses
1st Reading			
Responsorial			
2nd Reading			
Verse			
Gospel			

Notes

✠ Reflections ✠

Thank You Lord

Daily Reflections

My Jesus, I believe that You are present in the Most Holy Sacrament. I love You above all things, and I desire to receive You into my soul. Since I cannot at this moment receive You sacramentally, come at least spiritually into my heart. I embrace You as if You were already there and unite myself wholly to You. Never permit me to be separated from You. Amen.

Sunday		
Monday		
Tuesday		
Wednesday		
Thursday		
Friday		
Saturday		

The Spiritual Works of Mercy

To admonish sinners
To instruct the ignorant
To counsel the doubtful
To comfort the sorrowful
To bear wrongs patiently
To forgive all injuries
To pray for the living and the dead

I
T
r
u
s
t

J
e
s
u
s

The Corporal Works of Mercy

To feed the hungry
To give drink to the thirsty
To clothe the naked
To visit and ransom the captives
To shelter the homeless
To visit the sick
To bury the dead

Prayers & Answers

Date:	Date:
Prayer:	Prayer:
Answer:	Answer:

Daily Examination of Conscience

Sins:	Pride	Greed	Gluttony	Lust	Sloth	Envy	Anger
Virtues:	Humiliy	Generosity	Abstinence	Chastity	Diligence	Kindness	Patience

Sunday		
Monday		
Tuesday		
Wednesday		
Thursday		
Friday		
Saturday		

Act of Contrition

My God, I am sorry for my sins with all my heart. In
choosing to do wrong and failing to do good, I have
sinned against you whom I should love above all
things. I firmly intend, with your help, to do penance,
to sin no more, and to avoid whatever leads me to
sin. Our Savior Jesus Christ suffered and died for us.
In His name, my God, have mercy on us.

Mercy

Forgiveness

Amen.

Prayers & Answers

Date:	Date:
Prayer:	Prayer:
Answer:	Answer:

Reflections: Mass, Homily & Scriptures

Date:

	Book	Chapter	Verses
1st Reading			
Responsorial			
2nd Reading			
Verse			
Gospel			

Notes

☦ Reflections ☦

Thank You Lord

Daily Reflections

My Jesus, I believe that You are present in the Most Holy Sacrament. I love You above all things, and I desire to receive You into my soul. Since I cannot at this moment receive You sacramentally, come at least spiritually into my heart. I embrace You as if You were already there and unite myself wholly to You. Never permit me to be separated from You. Amen.

Sunday		
Monday		
Tuesday		
Wednesday		
Thursday		
Friday		
Saturday		

The Spiritual Works of Mercy

To admonish sinners
To instruct the ignorant
To counsel the doubtful
To comfort the sorrowful
To bear wrongs patiently
To forgive all injuries
To pray for the living and the dead

I T r u s t J e s u s

The Corporal Works of Mercy

To feed the hungry
To give drink to the thirsty
To clothe the naked
To visit and ransom the captives
To shelter the homeless
To visit the sick
To bury the dead

Prayers & Answers

Date:	Date:
Prayer:	Prayer:
Answer:	Answer:

Daily Examination of Conscience

Sins:	Pride	Greed	Gluttony	Lust	Sloth	Envy	Anger
Virtues:	Humily	Generosity	Abstinence	Chastity	Diligence	Kindness	Patience

Sunday		
Monday		
Tuesday		
Wednesday		
Thursday		
Friday		
Saturday		

Act of Contrition

M
e
r
c
y

My God, I am sorry for my sins with all my heart. In
choosing to do wrong and failing to do good, I have
sinned against you whom I should love above all
things. I firmly intend, with your help, to do penance,
to sin no more, and to avoid whatever leads me to
sin. Our Savior Jesus Christ suffered and died for us.
In His name, my God, have mercy on us.
Amen.

F
o
r
g
i
v
e
n
e
s
s

Prayers & Answers

Date:	Date:
Prayer:	Prayer:
Answer:	Answer:

Reflections: Mass, Homily & Scriptures

Date:

	Book	Chapter	Verses
1st Reading			
Responsorial			
2nd Reading			
Verse			
Gospel			

Notes

_____
_____
_____
_____
_____
_____
_____
_____
_____
_____
_____
_____
_____

✝ Reflections ✝

_____
_____
_____
_____
_____
_____
_____
_____
_____
_____
_____

Thank You Lord

Daily Reflections

My Jesus, I believe that You are present in the Most Holy Sacrament. I love You above all things, and I desire to receive You into my soul. Since I cannot at this moment receive You sacramentally, come at least spiritually into my heart. I embrace You as if You were already there and unite myself wholly to You. Never permit me to be separated from You. Amen.

Sunday		
Monday		
Tuesday		
Wednesday		
Thursday		
Friday		
Saturday		

The Spiritual Works of Mercy

To admonish sinners
To instruct the ignorant
To counsel the doubtful
To comfort the sorrowful
To bear wrongs patiently
To forgive all injuries
To pray for the living and the dead

I T r u s t J e s u s

The Corporal Works of Mercy

To feed the hungry
To give drink to the thirsty
To clothe the naked
To visit and ransom the captives
To shelter the homeless
To visit the sick
To bury the dead

Prayers & Answers

Date:	Date:
Prayer:	Prayer:
Answer:	Answer:

Daily Examination of Conscience

Sins:	Pride	Greed	Gluttony	Lust	Sloth	Envy	Anger
Virtues:	Humily	Generosity	Abstinence	Chastity	Diligence	Kindness	Patience

Sunday		
Monday		
Tuesday		
Wednesday		
Thursday		
Friday		
Saturday		

Act of Contrition

M
e
r
c
y

My God, I am sorry for my sins with all my heart. In choosing to do wrong and failing to do good, I have sinned against you whom I should love above all things. I firmly intend, with your help, to do penance, to sin no more, and to avoid whatever leads me to sin. Our Savior Jesus Christ suffered and died for us. In His name, my God, have mercy on us.

F
o
r
g
i
v
e
n
e
s
s

Amen.

Prayers & Answers

Date:	Date:
Prayer:	Prayer:
Answer:	Answer:

Reflections: Mass, Homily & Scriptures

Date:

	Book	Chapter	Verses
1st Reading			
Responsorial			
2nd Reading			
Verse			
Gospel			

Notes

✠ Reflections ✠

Thank You Lord

Daily Reflections

My Jesus, I believe that You are present in the Most Holy Sacrament. I love You above all things, and I desire to receive You into my soul. Since I cannot at this moment receive You sacramentally, come at least spiritually into my heart. I embrace You as if You were already there and unite myself wholly to You. Never permit me to be separated from You. Amen.

Sunday		
Monday		
Tuesday		
Wednesday		
Thursday		
Friday		
Saturday		

The Spiritual Works of Mercy

To admonish sinners
To instruct the ignorant
To counsel the doubtful
To comfort the sorrowful
To bear wrongs patiently
To forgive all injuries
To pray for the living and the dead

I
T
r
u
s
t

J
e
s
u
s

The Corporal Works of Mercy

To feed the hungry
To give drink to the thirsty
To clothe the naked
To visit and ransom the captives
To shelter the homeless
To visit the sick
To bury the dead

Prayers & Answers

Date:	Date:
Prayer:	Prayer:
Answer:	Answer:

Daily Examination of Conscience

Sins:	Pride	Greed	Gluttony	Lust	Sloth	Envy	Anger
Virtues:	Humily	Generosity	Abstinence	Chastity	Diligence	Kindness	Patience

Sunday		
Monday		
Tuesday		
Wednesday		
Thursday		
Friday		
Saturday		

Act of Contrition

M
e
r
c
y

My God, I am sorry for my sins with all my heart. In choosing to do wrong and failing to do good, I have sinned against you whom I should love above all things. I firmly intend, with your help, to do penance, to sin no more, and to avoid whatever leads me to sin. Our Savior Jesus Christ suffered and died for us. In His name, my God, have mercy on us.

F
o
r
g
i
v
e
n
e
s
s

Amen.

Prayers & Answers

Date:	Date:
Prayer:	Prayer:
Answer:	Answer:

Reflections: Mass, Homily & Scriptures

Date:

	Book	Chapter	Verses
1st Reading			
Responsorial			
2nd Reading			
Verse			
Gospel			

Notes

✠ Reflections ✠

Thank You Lord

Daily Reflections

My Jesus, I believe that You are present in the Most Holy Sacrament. I love You above all things, and I desire to receive You into my soul. Since I cannot at this moment receive You sacramentally, come at least spiritually into my heart. I embrace You as if You were already there and unite myself wholly to You. Never permit me to be separated from You. Amen.

Sunday		
Monday		
Tuesday		
Wednesday		
Thursday		
Friday		
Saturday		

The Spiritual Works of Mercy

To admonish sinners
To instruct the ignorant
To counsel the doubtful
To comfort the sorrowful
To bear wrongs patiently
To forgive all injuries
To pray for the living and the dead

I
T
r
u
s
t

J
e
s
u
s

The Corporal Works of Mercy

To feed the hungry
To give drink to the thirsty
To clothe the naked
To visit and ransom the captives
To shelter the homeless
To visit the sick
To bury the dead

Prayers & Answers

Date:	Date:
Prayer:	Prayer:
Answer:	Answer:

Daily Examination of Conscience

Sins:	Pride	Greed	Gluttony	Lust	Sloth	Envy	Anger
Virtues:	Humily	Generosity	Abstinence	Chastity	Diligence	Kindness	Patience

Sunday		
Monday		
Tuesday		
Wednesday		
Thursday		
Friday		
Saturday		

Act of Contrition

M
e
r
c
y

My God, I am sorry for my sins with all my heart. In choosing to do wrong and failing to do good, I have sinned against you whom I should love above all things. I firmly intend, with your help, to do penance, to sin no more, and to avoid whatever leads me to sin. Our Savior Jesus Christ suffered and died for us. In His name, my God, have mercy on us.

F
o
r
g
i
v
e
n
e
s
s

Amen.

Prayers & Answers

Date:	Date:
Prayer:	Prayer:
Answer:	Answer:

And so with all the
Angels and the Saints...

Therefore I ask...to
pray for me

Guardian Angel Prayer

*Angel of God,
my guardian dear,
To whom God's love
commits me here,
Ever this day,
be at my side,
To light and guard,
Rule and guide.*

Amen.

Reflections: Mass, Homily & Scriptures

Date:

	Book	Chapter	Verses
1st Reading			
Responsorial			
2nd Reading			
Verse			
Gospel			

Notes

✠ Reflections ✠

Thank You Lord

Daily Reflections

My Jesus, I believe that You are present in the Most Holy Sacrament. I love You above all things, and I desire to receive You into my soul. Since I cannot at this moment receive You sacramentally, come at least spiritually into my heart. I embrace You as if You were already there and unite myself wholly to You. Never permit me to be separated from You. Amen.

Sunday		
Monday		
Tuesday		
Wednesday		
Thursday		
Friday		
Saturday		

The Spiritual Works of Mercy

To admonish sinners
To instruct the ignorant
To counsel the doubtful
To comfort the sorrowful
To bear wrongs patiently
To forgive all injuries
To pray for the living and the dead

I
T
r
u
s
t

J
e
s
u
s

The Corporal Works of Mercy

To feed the hungry
To give drink to the thirsty
To clothe the naked
To visit and ransom the captives
To shelter the homeless
To visit the sick
To bury the dead

Prayers & Answers

Date:	Date:
Prayer:	Prayer:
Answer:	Answer:

Daily Examination of Conscience

Sins:	Pride	Greed	Gluttony	Lust	Sloth	Envy	Anger
Virtues:	Humily	Generosity	Abstinence	Chastity	Diligence	Kindness	Patience

Sunday		
Monday		
Tuesday		
Wednesday		
Thursday		
Friday		
Saturday		

Act of Contrition

M
e
r
c
y

My God, I am sorry for my sins with all my heart. In
choosing to do wrong and failing to do good, I have
sinned against you whom I should love above all
things. I firmly intend, with your help, to do penance,
to sin no more, and to avoid whatever leads me to
sin. Our Savior Jesus Christ suffered and died for us.
In His name, my God, have mercy on us.

F
o
r
g
i
v
e
n
e
s
s

Amen.

Prayers & Answers

Date:	Date:
Prayer:	Prayer:
Answer:	Answer:

Reflections: Mass, Homily & Scriptures

Date:

	Book	Chapter	Verses
1st Reading			
Responsorial			
2nd Reading			
Verse			
Gospel			

Notes

☩ Reflections ☩

Thank You Lord

Daily Reflections

My Jesus, I believe that You are present in the Most Holy Sacrament. I love You above all things, and I desire to receive You into my soul. Since I cannot at this moment receive You sacramentally, come at least spiritually into my heart. I embrace You as if You were already there and unite myself wholly to You. Never permit me to be separated from You. Amen.

Sunday		
Monday		
Tuesday		
Wednesday		
Thursday		
Friday		
Saturday		

The Spiritual Works of Mercy

To admonish sinners
To instruct the ignorant
To counsel the doubtful
To comfort the sorrowful
To bear wrongs patiently
To forgive all injuries
To pray for the living and the dead

I T r u s t J e s u s

The Corporal Works of Mercy

To feed the hungry
To give drink to the thirsty
To clothe the naked
To visit and ransom the captives
To shelter the homeless
To visit the sick
To bury the dead

Prayers & Answers

Date:	Date:
Prayer:	Prayer:
Answer:	Answer:

Daily Examination of Conscience

Sins:	Pride	Greed	Gluttony	Lust	Sloth	Envy	Anger
Virtues:	Humily	Generosity	Abstinence	Chastity	Diligence	Kindness	Patience

Sunday		
Monday		
Tuesday		
Wednesday		
Thursday		
Friday		
Saturday		

Act of Contrition

M
e
r
c
y

My God, I am sorry for my sins with all my heart. In
choosing to do wrong and failing to do good, I have
sinned against you whom I should love above all
things. I firmly intend, with your help, to do penance,
to sin no more, and to avoid whatever leads me to
sin. Our Savior Jesus Christ suffered and died for us.
In His name, my God, have mercy on us.

Forgiveness

Amen.

Prayers & Answers

Date:	Date:
Prayer:	Prayer:
Answer:	Answer:

Reflections: Mass, Homily & Scriptures

Date:

	Book	Chapter	Verses
1st Reading			
Responsorial			
2nd Reading			
Verse			
Gospel			

Notes

✝ Reflections ✝

Thank You Lord

Daily Reflections

My Jesus, I believe that You are present in the Most Holy Sacrament. I love You above all things, and I desire to receive You into my soul. Since I cannot at this moment receive You sacramentally, come at least spiritually into my heart. I embrace You as if You were already there and unite myself wholly to You. Never permit me to be separated from You. Amen.

Sunday		
Monday		
Tuesday		
Wednesday		
Thursday		
Friday		
Saturday		

The Spiritual Works of Mercy

To admonish sinners
To instruct the ignorant
To counsel the doubtful
To comfort the sorrowful
To bear wrongs patiently
To forgive all injuries
To pray for the living and the dead

I
T
r
u
s
t

J
e
s
u
s

The Corporal Works of Mercy

To feed the hungry
To give drink to the thirsty
To clothe the naked
To visit and ransom the captives
To shelter the homeless
To visit the sick
To bury the dead

Prayers & Answers

Date:	Date:
Prayer:	Prayer:
Answer:	Answer:

Daily Examination of Conscience

Sins:	Pride	Greed	Gluttony	Lust	Sloth	Envy	Anger
Virtues:	Humily	Generosity	Abstinence	Chastity	Diligence	Kindness	Patience

Sunday		
Monday		
Tuesday		
Wednesday		
Thursday		
Friday		
Saturday		

Act of Contrition

M
e
r
c
y

My God, I am sorry for my sins with all my heart. In choosing to do wrong and failing to do good, I have sinned against you whom I should love above all things. I firmly intend, with your help, to do penance, to sin no more, and to avoid whatever leads me to sin. Our Savior Jesus Christ suffered and died for us. In His name, my God, have mercy on us.

F
o
r
g
i
v
e
n
e
s
s

Amen.

Prayers & Answers

Date:	Date:
Prayer:	Prayer:
Answer:	Answer:

Reflections: Mass, Homily & Scriptures

Date:

	Book	Chapter	Verses
1st Reading			
Responsorial			
2nd Reading			
Verse			
Gospel			

Notes

_____

_____

_____

_____

_____

_____

_____

_____

_____

_____

_____

_____

✠ Reflections ✠

_____

_____

_____

_____

_____

_____

_____

_____

_____

_____

_____

Thank You Lord

Daily Reflections

My Jesus, I believe that You are present in the Most Holy Sacrament. I love You above all things, and I desire to receive You into my soul. Since I cannot at this moment receive You sacramentally, come at least spiritually into my heart. I embrace You as if You were already there and unite myself wholly to You. Never permit me to be separated from You. Amen.

Sunday		
Monday		
Tuesday		
Wednesday		
Thursday		
Friday		
Saturday		

The Spiritual Works of Mercy

To admonish sinners
To instruct the ignorant
To counsel the doubtful
To comfort the sorrowful
To bear wrongs patiently
To forgive all injuries
To pray for the living and the dead

I T r u s t J e s u s

The Corporal Works of Mercy

To feed the hungry
To give drink to the thirsty
To clothe the naked
To visit and ransom the captives
To shelter the homeless
To visit the sick
To bury the dead

Prayers & Answers

Date:	Date:
Prayer:	Prayer:
Answer:	Answer:

Daily Examination of Conscience

Sins:	Pride	Greed	Gluttony	Lust	Sloth	Envy	Anger
Virtues:	Humily	Generosity	Abstinence	Chastity	Diligence	Kindness	Patience

Sunday		
Monday		
Tuesday		
Wednesday		
Thursday		
Friday		
Saturday		

Act of Contrition

M e r c y

My God, I am sorry for my sins with all my heart. In choosing to do wrong and failing to do good, I have sinned against you whom I should love above all things. I firmly intend, with your help, to do penance, to sin no more, and to avoid whatever leads me to sin. Our Savior Jesus Christ suffered and died for us. In His name, my God, have mercy on us.

Forgiveness

Amen.

Prayers & Answers

Date:	Date:
Prayer:	Prayer:
Answer:	Answer:

Reflections: Mass, Homily & Scriptures

Date:

	Book	Chapter	Verses
1st Reading			
Responsorial			
2nd Reading			
Verse			
Gospel			

Notes

✠ Reflections ✠

Thank You Lord

Daily Reflections

My Jesus, I believe that You are present in the Most Holy Sacrament. I love You above all things, and I desire to receive You into my soul. Since I cannot at this moment receive You sacramentally, come at least spiritually into my heart. I embrace You as if You were already there and unite myself wholly to You. Never permit me to be separated from You. Amen.

Sunday		
Monday		
Tuesday		
Wednesday		
Thursday		
Friday		
Saturday		

The Spiritual Works of Mercy	I T r u s t	The Corporal Works of Mercy
To admonish sinners		To feed the hungry
To instruct the ignorant		To give drink to the thirsty
To counsel the doubtful		To clothe the naked
To comfort the sorrowful	J e s u s	To visit and ransom the captives
To bear wrongs patiently		To shelter the homeless
To forgive all injuries		To visit the sick
To pray for the living and the dead		To bury the dead

Prayers & Answers

Date:	Date:
Prayer:	Prayer:
Answer:	Answer:

Daily Examination of Conscience

Sins:	Pride	Greed	Gluttony	Lust	Sloth	Envy	Anger
Virtues:	Humily	Generosity	Abstinence	Chastity	Diligence	Kindness	Patience

Sunday		
Monday		
Tuesday		
Wednesday		
Thursday		
Friday		
Saturday		

Act of Contrition

M
e
r
c
y

My God, I am sorry for my sins with all my heart. In
choosing to do wrong and failing to do good, I have
sinned against you whom I should love above all
things. I firmly intend, with your help, to do penance,
to sin no more, and to avoid whatever leads me to
sin. Our Savior Jesus Christ suffered and died for us.
In His name, my God, have mercy on us.

F
o
r
g
i
v
e
n
e
s
s

Amen.

Prayers & Answers

Date:	Date:
Prayer:	Prayer:
Answer:	Answer:

Like the dewfall…

For through your
goodness we have
received…

Hail Mary

Hail Mary,
Full of Grace,
The Lord is with thee.
Blessed art thou among women,
and blessed is the fruit
of thy womb, Jesus.
Holy Mary,
Mother of God,
pray for us sinners now,
and at the hour of death.

Amen.

Reflections: Mass, Homily & Scriptures

Date:

	Book	Chapter	Verses
1st Reading			
Responsorial			
2nd Reading			
Verse			
Gospel			

Notes

✠ Reflections ✠

Thank You Lord

Daily Reflections

My Jesus, I believe that You are present in the Most Holy Sacrament. I love You above all things, and I desire to receive You into my soul. Since I cannot at this moment receive You sacramentally, come at least spiritually into my heart. I embrace You as if You were already there and unite myself wholly to You. Never permit me to be separated from You. Amen.

Sunday		
Monday		
Tuesday		
Wednesday		
Thursday		
Friday		
Saturday		

The Spiritual Works of Mercy

To admonish sinners
To instruct the ignorant
To counsel the doubtful
To comfort the sorrowful
To bear wrongs patiently
To forgive all injuries
To pray for the living and the dead

The Corporal Works of Mercy

To feed the hungry
To give drink to the thirsty
To clothe the naked
To visit and ransom the captives
To shelter the homeless
To visit the sick
To bury the dead

Prayers & Answers

Date:	Date:
Prayer:	Prayer:
Answer:	Answer:

Daily Examination of Conscience

Sins:	Pride	Greed	Gluttony	Lust	Sloth	Envy	Anger
Virtues:	Humily	Generosity	Abstinence	Chastity	Diligence	Kindness	Patience

Sunday		
Monday		
Tuesday		
Wednesday		
Thursday		
Friday		
Saturday		

Act of Contrition

M
e
r
c
y

My God, I am sorry for my sins with all my heart. In choosing to do wrong and failing to do good, I have sinned against you whom I should love above all things. I firmly intend, with your help, to do penance, to sin no more, and to avoid whatever leads me to sin. Our Savior Jesus Christ suffered and died for us. In His name, my God, have mercy on us.

F
o
r
g
i
v
e
n
e
s
s

Amen.

Prayers & Answers

Date:	Date:
Prayer:	Prayer:
Answer:	Answer:

Reflections: Mass, Homily & Scriptures

Date:

	Book	Chapter	Verses
1st Reading			
Responsorial			
2nd Reading			
Verse			
Gospel			

Notes

✠ Reflections ✠

Thank You Lord

Daily Reflections

My Jesus, I believe that You are present in the Most Holy Sacrament. I love You above all things, and I desire to receive You into my soul. Since I cannot at this moment receive You sacramentally, come at least spiritually into my heart. I embrace You as if You were already there and unite myself wholly to You. Never permit me to be separated from You. Amen.

Sunday		
Monday		
Tuesday		
Wednesday		
Thursday		
Friday		
Saturday		

The Spiritual Works of Mercy

To admonish sinners
To instruct the ignorant
To counsel the doubtful
To comfort the sorrowful
To bear wrongs patiently
To forgive all injuries
To pray for the living and the dead

The Corporal Works of Mercy

To feed the hungry
To give drink to the thirsty
To clothe the naked
To visit and ransom the captives
To shelter the homeless
To visit the sick
To bury the dead

Prayers & Answers

Date:	Date:
Prayer:	Prayer:
Answer:	Answer:

Daily Examination of Conscience

Sins:	Pride	Greed	Gluttony	Lust	Sloth	Envy	Anger
Virtues:	Humily	Generosity	Abstinence	Chastity	Diligence	Kindness	Patience

Sunday		
Monday		
Tuesday		
Wednesday		
Thursday		
Friday		
Saturday		

Act of Contrition

M
e
r
c
y

My God, I am sorry for my sins with all my heart. In
choosing to do wrong and failing to do good, I have
sinned against you whom I should love above all
things. I firmly intend, with your help, to do penance,
to sin no more, and to avoid whatever leads me to
sin. Our Savior Jesus Christ suffered and died for us.
In His name, my God, have mercy on us.

Forgivenesss

Amen.

Prayers & Answers

Date:	Date:
Prayer:	Prayer:
Answer:	Answer:

Reflections: Mass, Homily & Scriptures

Date:

	Book	Chapter	Verses
1st Reading			
Responsorial			
2nd Reading			
Verse			
Gospel			

Notes

✠ Reflections ✠

Thank You Lord

Daily Reflections

My Jesus, I believe that You are present in the Most Holy Sacrament. I love You above all things, and I desire to receive You into my soul. Since I cannot at this moment receive You sacramentally, come at least spiritually into my heart. I embrace You as if You were already there and unite myself wholly to You. Never permit me to be separated from You. Amen.

Sunday		
Monday		
Tuesday		
Wednesday		
Thursday		
Friday		
Saturday		

The Spiritual Works of Mercy

To admonish sinners
To instruct the ignorant
To counsel the doubtful
To comfort the sorrowful
To bear wrongs patiently
To forgive all injuries
To pray for the living and the dead

The Corporal Works of Mercy

To feed the hungry
To give drink to the thirsty
To clothe the naked
To visit and ransom the captives
To shelter the homeless
To visit the sick
To bury the dead

Trust Jesus

Prayers & Answers

Date:	Date:
Prayer:	Prayer:
Answer:	Answer:

Daily Examination of Conscience

Sins:	Pride	Greed	Gluttony	Lust	Sloth	Envy	Anger
Virtues:	Humily	Generosity	Abstinence	Chastity	Diligence	Kindness	Patience

Sunday		
Monday		
Tuesday		
Wednesday		
Thursday		
Friday		
Saturday		

Act of Contrition

M
c
r
c
y

My God, I am sorry for my sins with all my heart. In
choosing to do wrong and failing to do good, I have
sinned against you whom I should love above all
things. I firmly intend, with your help, to do penance,
to sin no more, and to avoid whatever leads me to
sin. Our Savior Jesus Christ suffered and died for us.
In His name, my God, have mercy on us.

F
o
r
g
i
v
e
n
e
s
s

Amen.

Prayers & Answers

Date:	Date:
Prayer:	Prayer:
Answer:	Answer:

Reflections: Mass, Homily & Scriptures

Date:

	Book	Chapter	Verses
1st Reading			
Responsorial			
2nd Reading			
Verse			
Gospel			

Notes

✝ Reflections ✝

Thank You Lord

Daily Reflections

My Jesus, I believe that You are present in the Most Holy Sacrament. I love You above all things, and I desire to receive You into my soul. Since I cannot at this moment receive You sacramentally, come at least spiritually into my heart. I embrace You as if You were already there and unite myself wholly to You. Never permit me to be separated from You. Amen.

Sunday		
Monday		
Tuesday		
Wednesday		
Thursday		
Friday		
Saturday		

The Spiritual Works of Mercy

To admonish sinners
To instruct the ignorant
To counsel the doubtful
To comfort the sorrowful
To bear wrongs patiently
To forgive all injuries
To pray for the living and the dead

I T r u s t   J e s u s

The Corporal Works of Mercy

To feed the hungry
To give drink to the thirsty
To clothe the naked
To visit and ransom the captives
To shelter the homeless
To visit the sick
To bury the dead

Prayers & Answers

Date:	Date:
Prayer:	Prayer:
Answer:	Answer:

Daily Examination of Conscience

Sins:	Pride	Greed	Gluttony	Lust	Sloth	Envy	Anger
Virtues:	Humily	Generosity	Abstinence	Chastity	Diligence	Kindness	Patience

Sunday		
Monday		
Tuesday		
Wednesday		
Thursday		
Friday		
Saturday		

Act of Contrition

M
e
r
c
y
.

My God, I am sorry for my sins with all my heart. In choosing to do wrong and failing to do good, I have sinned against you whom I should love above all things. I firmly intend, with your help, to do penance, to sin no more, and to avoid whatever leads me to sin. Our Savior Jesus Christ suffered and died for us. In His name, my God, have mercy on us.

F
o
r
g
i
v
e
n
e
s
s

Amen.

Prayers & Answers

Date:	Date:
Prayer:	Prayer:
Answer:	Answer:

Reflections: Mass, Homily & Scriptures

Date:

	Book	Chapter	Verses
1st Reading			
Responsorial			
2nd Reading			
Verse			
Gospel			

Notes

✠ Reflections ✠

Thank You Lord

Daily Reflections

My Jesus, I believe that You are present in the Most Holy Sacrament. I love You above all things, and I desire to receive You into my soul. Since I cannot at this moment receive You sacramentally, come at least spiritually into my heart. I embrace You as if You were already there and unite myself wholly to You. Never permit me to be separated from You. Amen.

Sunday		
Monday		
Tuesday		
Wednesday		
Thursday		
Friday		
Saturday		

The Spiritual Works of Mercy

To admonish sinners
To instruct the ignorant
To counsel the doubtful
To comfort the sorrowful
To bear wrongs patiently
To forgive all injuries
To pray for the living and the dead

I
T
r
u
s
t

J
e
s
u
s

The Corporal Works of Mercy

To feed the hungry
To give drink to the thirsty
To clothe the naked
To visit and ransom the captives
To shelter the homeless
To visit the sick
To bury the dead

Prayers & Answers

Date:	Date:
Prayer:	Prayer:
Answer:	Answer:

Daily Examination of Conscience

Sins:	Pride	Greed	Gluttony	Lust	Sloth	Envy	Anger
Virtues:	Humily	Generosity	Abstinence	Chastity	Diligence	Kindness	Patience

Sunday		
Monday		
Tuesday		
Wednesday		
Thursday		
Friday		
Saturday		

Act of Contrition

M
e
r
c
y

My God, I am sorry for my sins with all my heart. In
choosing to do wrong and failing to do good, I have
sinned against you whom I should love above all
things. I firmly intend, with your help, to do penance,
to sin no more, and to avoid whatever leads me to
sin. Our Savior Jesus Christ suffered and died for us.
In His name, my God, have mercy on us.

F
o
r
g
i
v
e
n
e
s
s

Amen.

Prayers & Answers

Date:	Date:
Prayer:	Prayer:
Answer:	Answer:

You have done great things…

When you looked on
the lowliness of your
handmaid…

Memorare

*Remember, O most gracious Virgin Mary, that
never was it known that anyone who fled to thy
protection, implored thy help, or sought thine
intercession was left unaided.*

*Inspired by this confidence, I fly unto thee, O
Virgin of virgins, my mother; to thee do I come,
before thee I stand, sinful and sorrowful. O
Mother of the Word Incarnate, despise not my
petitions, but in thy mercy hear and answer me.*

Amen.

Reflections: Mass, Homily & Scriptures

Date:

	Book	Chapter	Verses
1st Reading			
Responsorial			
2nd Reading			
Verse			
Gospel			

Notes

✝ Reflections ✝

Thank You Lord

Daily Reflections

My Jesus, I believe that You are present in the Most Holy Sacrament. I love You above all things, and I desire to receive You into my soul. Since I cannot at this moment receive You sacramentally, come at least spiritually into my heart. I embrace You as if You were already there and unite myself wholly to You. Never permit me to be separated from You. Amen.

Sunday		
Monday		
Tuesday		
Wednesday		
Thursday		
Friday		
Saturday		

The Spiritual Works of Mercy

To admonish sinners
To instruct the ignorant
To counsel the doubtful
To comfort the sorrowful
To bear wrongs patiently
To forgive all injuries
To pray for the living and the dead

The Corporal Works of Mercy

To feed the hungry
To give drink to the thirsty
To clothe the naked
To visit and ransom the captives
To shelter the homeless
To visit the sick
To bury the dead

Prayers & Answers

Date:	Date:
Prayer:	Prayer:
Answer:	Answer:

Daily Examination of Conscience

Sins:	Pride	Greed	Gluttony	Lust	Sloth	Envy	Anger
Virtues:	Humily	Generosity	Abstinence	Chastity	Diligence	Kindness	Patience

Sunday		
Monday		
Tuesday		
Wednesday		
Thursday		
Friday		
Saturday		

Act of Contrition

M
e
r
c
y

My God, I am sorry for my sins with all my heart. In
choosing to do wrong and failing to do good, I have
sinned against you whom I should love above all
things. I firmly intend, with your help, to do penance,
to sin no more, and to avoid whatever leads me to
sin. Our Savior Jesus Christ suffered and died for us.
In His name, my God, have mercy on us.

F
o
r
g
i
v
e
n
e
s
s

Amen.

Prayers & Answers

Date:	Date:
Prayer:	Prayer:
Answer:	Answer:

Reflections: Mass, Homily & Scriptures

Date:

	Book	Chapter	Verses
1st Reading			
Responsorial			
2nd Reading			
Verse			
Gospel			

Notes

✠ Reflections ✠

Thank You Lord

Daily Reflections

My Jesus, I believe that You are present in the Most Holy Sacrament. I love You above all things, and I desire to receive You into my soul. Since I cannot at this moment receive You sacramentally, come at least spiritually into my heart. I embrace You as if You were already there and unite myself wholly to You. Never permit me to be separated from You. Amen.

Sunday		
Monday		
Tuesday		
Wednesday		
Thursday		
Friday		
Saturday		

The Spiritual Works of Mercy

To admonish sinners
To instruct the ignorant
To counsel the doubtful
To comfort the sorrowful
To bear wrongs patiently
To forgive all injuries
To pray for the living and the dead

I T r u s t

J e s u s

The Corporal Works of Mercy

To feed the hungry
To give drink to the thirsty
To clothe the naked
To visit and ransom the captives
To shelter the homeless
To visit the sick
To bury the dead

Prayers & Answers

Date:	Date:
Prayer:	Prayer:
Answer:	Answer:

Daily Examination of Conscience

Sins:	Pride	Greed	Gluttony	Lust	Sloth	Envy	Anger
Virtues:	Humily	Generosity	Abstinence	Chastity	Diligence	Kindness	Patience

Sunday		
Monday		
Tuesday		
Wednesday		
Thursday		
Friday		
Saturday		

Act of Contrition

M
e
r
c
y

My God, I am sorry for my sins with all my heart. In
choosing to do wrong and failing to do good, I have
sinned against you whom I should love above all
things. I firmly intend, with your help, to do penance,
to sin no more, and to avoid whatever leads me to
sin. Our Savior Jesus Christ suffered and died for us.
In His name, my God, have mercy on us.

Forgiveness

Amen.

Prayers & Answers

Date:	Date:
Prayer:	Prayer:
Answer:	Answer:

Reflections: Mass, Homily & Scriptures

Date:

	Book	Chapter	Verses
1st Reading			
Responsorial			
2nd Reading			
Verse			
Gospel			

Notes

✞ Reflections ✞

Thank You Lord

Daily Reflections

My Jesus, I believe that You are present in the Most Holy Sacrament. I love You above all things, and I desire to receive You into my soul. Since I cannot at this moment receive You sacramentally, come at least spiritually into my heart. I embrace You as if You were already there and unite myself wholly to You. Never permit me to be separated from You. Amen.

Sunday		
Monday		
Tuesday		
Wednesday		
Thursday		
Friday		
Saturday		

The Spiritual Works of Mercy

To admonish sinners
To instruct the ignorant
To counsel the doubtful
To comfort the sorrowful
To bear wrongs patiently
To forgive all injuries
To pray for the living and the dead

I T r u s t

J e s u s

The Corporal Works of Mercy

To feed the hungry
To give drink to the thirsty
To clothe the naked
To visit and ransom the captives
To shelter the homeless
To visit the sick
To bury the dead

Prayers & Answers

Date:	Date:
Prayer:	Prayer:
Answer:	Answer:

Daily Examination of Conscience

Sins:	Pride	Greed	Gluttony	Lust	Sloth	Envy	Anger
Virtues:	Humily	Generosity	Abstinence	Chastity	Diligence	Kindness	Patience

Sunday		
Monday		
Tuesday		
Wednesday		
Thursday		
Friday		
Saturday		

Act of Contrition

M
e
r
c
y

My God, I am sorry for my sins with all my heart. In
choosing to do wrong and failing to do good, I have
sinned against you whom I should love above all
things. I firmly intend, with your help, to do penance,
to sin no more, and to avoid whatever leads me to
sin. Our Savior Jesus Christ suffered and died for us.
In His name, my God, have mercy on us.

F
o
r
g
i
v
e
n
e
s
s

Amen.

Prayers & Answers

Date:	Date:
Prayer:	Prayer:
Answer:	Answer:

Reflections: Mass, Homily & Scriptures

Date:

	Book	Chapter	Verses
1st Reading			
Responsorial			
2nd Reading			
Verse			
Gospel			

Notes

✠ Reflections ✠

Thank You Lord

Daily Reflections

My Jesus, I believe that You are present in the Most Holy Sacrament. I love You above all things, and I desire to receive You into my soul. Since I cannot at this moment receive You sacramentally, come at least spiritually into my heart. I embrace You as if You were already there and unite myself wholly to You. Never permit me to be separated from You. Amen.

Sunday		
Monday		
Tuesday		
Wednesday		
Thursday		
Friday		
Saturday		

The Spiritual Works of Mercy

To admonish sinners
To instruct the ignorant
To counsel the doubtful
To comfort the sorrowful
To bear wrongs patiently
To forgive all injuries
To pray for the living and the dead

I T r u s t J e s u s

The Corporal Works of Mercy

To feed the hungry
To give drink to the thirsty
To clothe the naked
To visit and ransom the captives
To shelter the homeless
To visit the sick
To bury the dead

Prayers & Answers

Date:	Date:
Prayer:	Prayer:
Answer:	Answer:

Daily Examination of Conscience

Sins:	Pride	Greed	Gluttony	Lust	Sloth	Envy	Anger
Virtues:	Humilty	Generosity	Abstinence	Chastity	Diligence	Kindness	Patience

Sunday		
Monday		
Tuesday		
Wednesday		
Thursday		
Friday		
Saturday		

Act of Contrition

M
e
r
c
y

My God, I am sorry for my sins with all my heart. In
choosing to do wrong and failing to do good, I have
sinned against you whom I should love above all
things. I firmly intend, with your help, to do penance,
to sin no more, and to avoid whatever leads me to
sin. Our Savior Jesus Christ suffered and died for us.
In His name, my God, have mercy on us.

F
o
r
g
i
v
e
n
e
s
s

Amen.

Prayers & Answers

Date:	Date:
Prayer:	Prayer:
Answer:	Answer:

Reflections: Mass, Homily & Scriptures

Date:

	Book	Chapter	Verses
1st Reading			
Responsorial			
2nd Reading			
Verse			
Gospel			

Notes

_____
_____
_____
_____
_____
_____
_____
_____
_____
_____
_____
_____

✠ Reflections ✠

_____
_____
_____
_____
_____
_____
_____
_____
_____
_____

Thank You Lord

Daily Reflections

My Jesus, I believe that You are present in the Most Holy Sacrament. I love You above all things, and I desire to receive You into my soul. Since I cannot at this moment receive You sacramentally, come at least spiritually into my heart. I embrace You as if You were already there and unite myself wholly to You. Never permit me to be separated from You. Amen.

Sunday		
Monday		
Tuesday		
Wednesday		
Thursday		
Friday		
Saturday		

The Spiritual Works of Mercy	I T r u s t	The Corporal Works of Mercy
To admonish sinners		To feed the hungry
To instruct the ignorant		To give drink to the thirsty
To counsel the doubtful	J e s u s	To clothe the naked
To comfort the sorrowful		To visit and ransom the captives
To bear wrongs patiently		To shelter the homeless
To forgive all injuries		To visit the sick
To pray for the living and the dead		To bury the dead

Prayers & Answers

Date:	Date:
Prayer:	Prayer:
Answer:	Answer:

Daily Examination of Conscience

Sins:	Pride	Greed	Gluttony	Lust	Sloth	Envy	Anger
Virtues:	Humily	Generosity	Abstinence	Chastity	Diligence	Kindness	Patience

Sunday		
Monday		
Tuesday		
Wednesday		
Thursday		
Friday		
Saturday		

Act of Contrition

M
e
r
c
y

My God, I am sorry for my sins with all my heart. In choosing to do wrong and failing to do good, I have sinned against you whom I should love above all things. I firmly intend, with your help, to do penance, to sin no more, and to avoid whatever leads me to sin. Our Savior Jesus Christ suffered and died for us. In His name, my God, have mercy on us.

F
o
r
g
i
v
e
n
e
s
s

Amen.

Prayers & Answers

Date:	Date:
Prayer:	Prayer:
Answer:	Answer:

Bless the Lord, O my soul...

In one chorus of
exultant praise…

The Prayer of Mary

*"My soul proclaims the greatness of the Lord,
my spirit rejoices in God my Savior
For he has looked upon his handmaid's lowliness;
behold, from now on will all ages call me blessed.
The Mighty One has done great things for me,
and holy is his name.*

*His mercy is from age to age to those who fear him.
He has shown might with his arm,
dispersed the arrogant of mind and heart.*

*He has thrown down the rulers from their thrones
but lifted up the lowly.
The hungry he has filled with good things;
the rich he has sent away empty.*

*He has helped Israel his servant,
remembering his mercy,
according to his promise to our fathers,
to Abraham and to his descendants forever."*

Lk 1:46-55

Reflections: Mass, Homily & Scriptures

Date:

	Book	Chapter	Verses
1st Reading			
Responsorial			
2nd Reading			
Verse			
Gospel			

Notes

✟ Reflections ✟

Thank You Lord

Daily Reflections

My Jesus, I believe that You are present in the Most Holy Sacrament. I love You above all things, and I desire to receive You into my soul. Since I cannot at this moment receive You sacramentally, come at least spiritually into my heart. I embrace You as if You were already there and unite myself wholly to You. Never permit me to be separated from You. Amen.

Sunday		
Monday		
Tuesday		
Wednesday		
Thursday		
Friday		
Saturday		

The Spiritual Works of Mercy

To admonish sinners
To instruct the ignorant
To counsel the doubtful
To comfort the sorrowful
To bear wrongs patiently
To forgive all injuries
To pray for the living and the dead

I
T
r
u
s
t

J
e
s
u
s

The Corporal Works of Mercy

To feed the hungry
To give drink to the thirsty
To clothe the naked
To visit and ransom the captives
To shelter the homeless
To visit the sick
To bury the dead

Prayers & Answers

Date:	Date:
Prayer:	Prayer:
Answer:	Answer:

Daily Examination of Conscience

Sins:	Pride	Greed	Gluttony	Lust	Sloth	Envy	Anger
Virtues:	Humily	Generosity	Abstinence	Chastity	Diligence	Kindness	Patience

Sunday		
Monday		
Tuesday		
Wednesday		
Thursday		
Friday		
Saturday		

Act of Contrition

M   My God, I am sorry for my sins with all my heart. In
e   choosing to do wrong and failing to do good, I have
r   sinned against you whom I should love above all
c   things. I firmly intend, with your help, to do penance,
y   to sin no more, and to avoid whatever leads me to
sin. Our Savior Jesus Christ suffered and died for us.
In His name, my God, have mercy on us.

Forgiveness

Amen.

Prayers & Answers

Date:	Date:
Prayer:	Prayer:
Answer:	Answer:

Reflections: Mass, Homily & Scriptures

Date:

	Book	Chapter	Verses
1st Reading			
Responsorial			
2nd Reading			
Verse			
Gospel			

Notes

_____
_____
_____
_____
_____
_____
_____
_____
_____
_____
_____
_____
_____

☩ Reflections ☩

_____
_____
_____
_____
_____
_____
_____
_____
_____
_____
_____
_____

Thank You Lord

Daily Reflections

My Jesus, I believe that You are present in the Most Holy Sacrament. I love You above all things, and I desire to receive You into my soul. Since I cannot at this moment receive You sacramentally, come at least spiritually into my heart. I embrace You as if You were already there and unite myself wholly to You. Never permit me to be separated from You. Amen.

Sunday		
Monday		
Tuesday		
Wednesday		
Thursday		
Friday		
Saturday		

The Spiritual Works of Mercy		The Corporal Works of Mercy
	I	
	T	
To admonish sinners	r	To feed the hungry
To instruct the ignorant	u	To give drink to the thirsty
To counsel the doubtful	s	To clothe the naked
To comfort the sorrowful	t	To visit and ransom the captives
To bear wrongs patiently	J	To shelter the homeless
To forgive all injuries	e	To visit the sick
To pray for the living and the dead	s	To bury the dead
	u	
	s	

Prayers & Answers

Date:	Date:
Prayer:	Prayer:
Answer:	Answer:

Daily Examination of Conscience

Sins:	Pride	Greed	Gluttony	Lust	Sloth	Envy	Anger
Virtues:	Humily	Generosity	Abstinence	Chastity	Diligence	Kindness	Patience

Sunday		
Monday		
Tuesday		
Wednesday		
Thursday		
Friday		
Saturday		

Act of Contrition

M
e
r
c
y

My God, I am sorry for my sins with all my heart. In
choosing to do wrong and failing to do good, I have
sinned against you whom I should love above all
things. I firmly intend, with your help, to do penance,
to sin no more, and to avoid whatever leads me to
sin. Our Savior Jesus Christ suffered and died for us.
In His name, my God, have mercy on us.

F
o
r
g
i
v
e
n
e
s
s

Amen.

Prayers & Answers

Date:	Date:
Prayer:	Prayer:
Answer:	Answer:

Reflections: Mass, Homily & Scriptures

Date:

	Book	Chapter	Verses
1st Reading			
Responsorial			
2nd Reading			
Verse			
Gospel			

Notes

✝ Reflections ✝

Thank You Lord

Daily Reflections

My Jesus, I believe that You are present in the Most Holy Sacrament. I love You above all things, and I desire to receive You into my soul. Since I cannot at this moment receive You sacramentally, come at least spiritually into my heart. I embrace You as if You were already there and unite myself wholly to You. Never permit me to be separated from You. Amen.

Sunday		
Monday		
Tuesday		
Wednesday		
Thursday		
Friday		
Saturday		

The Spiritual Works of Mercy	I T r u s t	The Corporal Works of Mercy
To admonish sinners		To feed the hungry
To instruct the ignorant		To give drink to the thirsty
To counsel the doubtful		To clothe the naked
To comfort the sorrowful	J e s u s	To visit and ransom the captives
To bear wrongs patiently		To shelter the homeless
To forgive all injuries		To visit the sick
To pray for the living and the dead		To bury the dead

Prayers & Answers

Date:	Date:
Prayer:	Prayer:
Answer:	Answer:

Daily Examination of Conscience

Sins:	Pride	Greed	Gluttony	Lust	Sloth	Envy	Anger
Virtues:	Humily	Generosity	Abstinence	Chastity	Diligence	Kindness	Patience

Sunday		
Monday		
Tuesday		
Wednesday		
Thursday		
Friday		
Saturday		

Act of Contrition

M
e
r
c
y

My God, I am sorry for my sins with all my heart. In choosing to do wrong and failing to do good, I have sinned against you whom I should love above all things. I firmly intend, with your help, to do penance, to sin no more, and to avoid whatever leads me to sin. Our Savior Jesus Christ suffered and died for us. In His name, my God, have mercy on us.

F
o
r
g
i
v
e
n
e
s
s

Amen.

Prayers & Answers

Date:	Date:
Prayer:	Prayer:
Answer:	Answer:

Reflections: Mass, Homily & Scriptures

Date:

	Book	Chapter	Verses
1st Reading			
Responsorial			
2nd Reading			
Verse			
Gospel			

Notes

✚ Reflections ✚

Thank You Lord

Daily Reflections

My Jesus, I believe that You are present in the Most Holy Sacrament. I love You above all things, and I desire to receive You into my soul. Since I cannot at this moment receive You sacramentally, come at least spiritually into my heart. I embrace You as if You were already there and unite myself wholly to You. Never permit me to be separated from You. Amen.

Sunday		
Monday		
Tuesday		
Wednesday		
Thursday		
Friday		
Saturday		

The Spiritual Works of Mercy

To admonish sinners
To instruct the ignorant
To counsel the doubtful
To comfort the sorrowful
To bear wrongs patiently
To forgive all injuries
To pray for the living and the dead

The Corporal Works of Mercy

To feed the hungry
To give drink to the thirsty
To clothe the naked
To visit and ransom the captives
To shelter the homeless
To visit the sick
To bury the dead

I T r u s t   J e s u s

Prayers & Answers

Date:	Date:
Prayer:	Prayer:
Answer:	Answer:

Daily Examination of Conscience

Sins:	Pride	Greed	Gluttony	Lust	Sloth	Envy	Anger
Virtues:	Humily	Generosity	Abstinence	Chastity	Diligence	Kindness	Patience

Sunday		
Monday		
Tuesday		
Wednesday		
Thursday		
Friday		
Saturday		

Act of Contrition

M
e
r
c
y

My God, I am sorry for my sins with all my heart. In choosing to do wrong and failing to do good, I have sinned against you whom I should love above all things. I firmly intend, with your help, to do penance, to sin no more, and to avoid whatever leads me to sin. Our Savior Jesus Christ suffered and died for us. In His name, my God, have mercy on us.

F
o
r
g
i
v
e
n
e
s
s

Amen.

Prayers & Answers

Date:	Date:
Prayer:	Prayer:
Answer:	Answer:

Reflections: Mass, Homily & Scriptures

Date:

	Book	Chapter	Verses
1st Reading			
Responsorial			
2nd Reading			
Verse			
Gospel			

Notes

✝ Reflections ✝

Thank You Lord

Daily Reflections

My Jesus, I believe that You are present in the Most Holy Sacrament. I love You above all things, and I desire to receive You into my soul. Since I cannot at this moment receive You sacramentally, come at least spiritually into my heart. I embrace You as if You were already there and unite myself wholly to You. Never permit me to be separated from You. Amen.

Sunday		
Monday		
Tuesday		
Wednesday		
Thursday		
Friday		
Saturday		

The Spiritual Works of Mercy

To admonish sinners
To instruct the ignorant
To counsel the doubtful
To comfort the sorrowful
To bear wrongs patiently
To forgive all injuries
To pray for the living and the dead

Trust Jesus

The Corporal Works of Mercy

To feed the hungry
To give drink to the thirsty
To clothe the naked
To visit and ransom the captives
To shelter the homeless
To visit the sick
To bury the dead

Prayers & Answers

Date:	Date:
Prayer:	Prayer:
Answer:	Answer:

Daily Examination of Conscience

Sins:	Pride	Greed	Gluttony	Lust	Sloth	Envy	Anger
Virtues:	Humily	Generosity	Abstinence	Chastity	Diligence	Kindness	Patience

Sunday		
Monday		
Tuesday		
Wednesday		
Thursday		
Friday		
Saturday		

Act of Contrition

M
e
r
c
y

My God, I am sorry for my sins with all my heart. In
choosing to do wrong and failing to do good, I have
sinned against you whom I should love above all
things. I firmly intend, with your help, to do penance,
to sin no more, and to avoid whatever leads me to
sin. Our Savior Jesus Christ suffered and died for us.
In His name, my God, have mercy on us.

F
o
r
g
i
v
e
n
e
s
s

Amen.

Prayers & Answers

Date:	Date:
Prayer:	Prayer:
Answer:	Answer:

 May we merit to be coheirs to Eternal Life…

Have mercy on us…

Divine Mercy Chaplet

Eternal Father, I offer You the Body and Blood,
Soul and Divinity
of Your dearly beloved Son, Our Lord Jesus
Christ, in atonement
for our sins and those of the whole world.

'For the sake of His sorrowful Passion have mercy
on us and on the
whole world.

'Holy God, Holy Mighty One, Holy Immortal
One, have mercy on us
and on the whole world.

Reflections: Mass, Homily & Scriptures

Date:

	Book	Chapter	Verses
1st Reading			
Responsorial			
2nd Reading			
Verse			
Gospel			

Notes

_____
_____
_____
_____
_____
_____
_____
_____
_____
_____
_____
_____
_____

✠ Reflections ✠

_____
_____
_____
_____
_____
_____
_____
_____
_____
_____
_____
_____

Thank You Lord

Daily Reflections

My Jesus, I believe that You are present in the Most Holy Sacrament. I love You above all things, and I desire to receive You into my soul. Since I cannot at this moment receive You sacramentally, come at least spiritually into my heart. I embrace You as if You were already there and unite myself wholly to You. Never permit me to be separated from You. Amen.

Sunday		
Monday		
Tuesday		
Wednesday		
Thursday		
Friday		
Saturday		

The Spiritual Works of Mercy

To admonish sinners
To instruct the ignorant
To counsel the doubtful
To comfort the sorrowful
To bear wrongs patiently
To forgive all injuries
To pray for the living and the dead

I
T
r
u
s
t

J
e
s
u
s

The Corporal Works of Mercy

To feed the hungry
To give drink to the thirsty
To clothe the naked
To visit and ransom the captives
To shelter the homeless
To visit the sick
To bury the dead

Prayers & Answers

Date:	Date:
Prayer:	Prayer:
Answer:	Answer:

Daily Examination of Conscience

Sins:	Pride	Greed	Gluttony	Lust	Sloth	Envy	Anger
Virtues:	Humily	Generosity	Abstinence	Chastity	Diligence	Kindness	Patience

Sunday		
Monday		
Tuesday		
Wednesday		
Thursday		
Friday		
Saturday		

Act of Contrition

M
e
r
c
y

F
o
r
g
i
v
e
n
e
s
s

My God, I am sorry for my sins with all my heart. In choosing to do wrong and failing to do good, I have sinned against you whom I should love above all things. I firmly intend, with your help, to do penance, to sin no more, and to avoid whatever leads me to sin. Our Savior Jesus Christ suffered and died for us. In His name, my God, have mercy on us.

Amen.

Prayers & Answers

Date:	Date:
Prayer:	Prayer:
Answer:	Answer:

Reflections: Mass, Homily & Scriptures

Date:

	Book	Chapter	Verses
1st Reading			
Responsorial			
2nd Reading			
Verse			
Gospel			

Notes

✠ Reflections ✠

Thank You Lord

Daily Reflections

My Jesus, I believe that You are present in the Most Holy Sacrament. I love You above all things, and I desire to receive You into my soul. Since I cannot at this moment receive You sacramentally, come at least spiritually into my heart. I embrace You as if You were already there and unite myself wholly to You. Never permit me to be separated from You. Amen.

Sunday		
Monday		
Tuesday		
Wednesday		
Thursday		
Friday		
Saturday		

The Spiritual Works of Mercy

To admonish sinners
To instruct the ignorant
To counsel the doubtful
To comfort the sorrowful
To bear wrongs patiently
To forgive all injuries
To pray for the living and the dead

I T r u s t

J e s u s

The Corporal Works of Mercy

To feed the hungry
To give drink to the thirsty
To clothe the naked
To visit and ransom the captives
To shelter the homeless
To visit the sick
To bury the dead

Prayers & Answers

Date:	Date:
Prayer:	Prayer:
Answer:	Answer:

Daily Examination of Conscience

Sins:	Pride	Greed	Gluttony	Lust	Sloth	Envy	Anger
Virtues:	Humily	Generosity	Abstinence	Chastity	Diligence	Kindness	Patience

Sunday		
Monday		
Tuesday		
Wednesday		
Thursday		
Friday		
Saturday		

Act of Contrition

M
e
r
c
y

My God, I am sorry for my sins with all my heart. In choosing to do wrong and failing to do good, I have sinned against you whom I should love above all things. I firmly intend, with your help, to do penance, to sin no more, and to avoid whatever leads me to sin. Our Savior Jesus Christ suffered and died for us. In His name, my God, have mercy on us.

F
o
r
g
i
v
e
n
e
s
s

Amen.

Prayers & Answers

Date:	Date:
Prayer:	Prayer:
Answer:	Answer:

Reflections: Mass, Homily & Scriptures

Date:

	Book	Chapter	Verses
1st Reading			
Responsorial			
2nd Reading			
Verse			
Gospel			

Notes

_____
_____
_____
_____
_____
_____
_____
_____
_____
_____
_____
_____

✝ Reflections ✝

_____
_____
_____
_____
_____
_____
_____
_____
_____
_____
_____

Thank You Lord

Daily Reflections

My Jesus, I believe that You are present in the Most Holy Sacrament. I love You above all things, and I desire to receive You into my soul. Since I cannot at this moment receive You sacramentally, come at least spiritually into my heart. I embrace You as if You were already there and unite myself wholly to You. Never permit me to be separated from You. Amen.

Sunday		
Monday		
Tuesday		
Wednesday		
Thursday		
Friday		
Saturday		

The Spiritual Works of Mercy

To admonish sinners
To instruct the ignorant
To counsel the doubtful
To comfort the sorrowful
To bear wrongs patiently
To forgive all injuries
To pray for the living and the dead

Jesus

The Corporal Works of Mercy

To feed the hungry
To give drink to the thirsty
To clothe the naked
To visit and ransom the captives
To shelter the homeless
To visit the sick
To bury the dead

Prayers & Answers

Date:	Date:
Prayer:	Prayer:
Answer:	Answer:

Daily Examination of Conscience

Sins:	Pride	Greed	Gluttony	Lust	Sloth	Envy	Anger
Virtues:	Humily	Generosity	Abstinence	Chastity	Diligence	Kindness	Patience

Sunday		
Monday		
Tuesday		
Wednesday		
Thursday		
Friday		
Saturday		

Act of Contrition

M
e
r
c
y

My God, I am sorry for my sins with all my heart. In choosing to do wrong and failing to do good, I have sinned against you whom I should love above all things. I firmly intend, with your help, to do penance, to sin no more, and to avoid whatever leads me to sin. Our Savior Jesus Christ suffered and died for us. In His name, my God, have mercy on us.

Amen.

F
o
r
g
i
v
e
n
e
s
s

Prayers & Answers

Date:	Date:
Prayer:	Prayer:
Answer:	Answer:

Reflections: Mass, Homily & Scriptures

Date:

	Book	Chapter	Verses
1st Reading			
Responsorial			
2nd Reading			
Verse			
Gospel			

Notes

✝ Reflections ✝

Thank You Lord

Daily Reflections

My Jesus, I believe that You are present in the Most Holy Sacrament. I love You above all things, and I desire to receive You into my soul. Since I cannot at this moment receive You sacramentally, come at least spiritually into my heart. I embrace You as if You were already there and unite myself wholly to You. Never permit me to be separated from You. Amen.

Sunday		
Monday		
Tuesday		
Wednesday		
Thursday		
Friday		
Saturday		

The Spiritual Works of Mercy

To admonish sinners
To instruct the ignorant
To counsel the doubtful
To comfort the sorrowful
To bear wrongs patiently
To forgive all injuries
To pray for the living and the dead

I T r u s t J e s u s

The Corporal Works of Mercy

To feed the hungry
To give drink to the thirsty
To clothe the naked
To visit and ransom the captives
To shelter the homeless
To visit the sick
To bury the dead

Prayers & Answers

Date:	Date:
Prayer:	Prayer:
Answer:	Answer:

Daily Examination of Conscience

Sins:	Pride	Greed	Gluttony	Lust	Sloth	Envy	Anger
Virtues:	Humily	Generosity	Abstinence	Chastity	Diligence	Kindness	Patience

Sunday		
Monday		
Tuesday		
Wednesday		
Thursday		
Friday		
Saturday		

Act of Contrition

M
e
r
c
y

My God, I am sorry for my sins with all my heart. In
choosing to do wrong and failing to do good, I have
sinned against you whom I should love above all
things. I firmly intend, with your help, to do penance,
to sin no more, and to avoid whatever leads me to
sin. Our Savior Jesus Christ suffered and died for us.
In His name, my God, have mercy on us.

F
o
r
g
i
v
e
n
e
s
s

Amen.

Prayers & Answers

Date:	Date:
Prayer:	Prayer:
Answer:	Answer:

Reflections: Mass, Homily & Scriptures

Date:

	Book	Chapter	Verses
1st Reading			
Responsorial			
2nd Reading			
Verse			
Gospel			

Notes

✝ Reflections ✝

Thank You Lord

Daily Reflections

My Jesus, I believe that You are present in the Most Holy Sacrament. I love You above all things, and I desire to receive You into my soul. Since I cannot at this moment receive You sacramentally, come at least spiritually into my heart. I embrace You as if You were already there and unite myself wholly to You. Never permit me to be separated from You. Amen.

Sunday		
Monday		
Tuesday		
Wednesday		
Thursday		
Friday		
Saturday		

The Spiritual Works of Mercy

To admonish sinners
To instruct the ignorant
To counsel the doubtful
To comfort the sorrowful
To bear wrongs patiently
To forgive all injuries
To pray for the living and the dead

The Corporal Works of Mercy

To feed the hungry
To give drink to the thirsty
To clothe the naked
To visit and ransom the captives
To shelter the homeless
To visit the sick
To bury the dead

Prayers & Answers

Date:	Date:
Prayer:	Prayer:
Answer:	Answer:

Daily Examination of Conscience

Sins:	Pride	Greed	Gluttony	Lust	Sloth	Envy	Anger
Virtues:	Humily	Generosity	Abstinence	Chastity	Diligence	Kindness	Patience

Sunday		
Monday		
Tuesday		
Wednesday		
Thursday		
Friday		
Saturday		

Act of Contrition

M
e
r
c
y

My God, I am sorry for my sins with all my heart. In
choosing to do wrong and failing to do good, I have
sinned against you whom I should love above all
things. I firmly intend, with your help, to do penance,
to sin no more, and to avoid whatever leads me to
sin. Our Savior Jesus Christ suffered and died for us.
In His name, my God, have mercy on us.

F
o
r
g
i
v
e
n
e
s
s

Amen.

Prayers & Answers

Date:	Date:
Prayer:	Prayer:
Answer:	Answer:

We may run as victors
in the race before us…

…win the imperishable
crown of glory

THE MYSTERIES OF THE ROSARY

THE JOYFUL MYSTERIES
(Mondays and Saturdays, and on Sundays during Advent and Christmas)

1. The Annunciation
2. The Visitation
3. The Nativity
4. The Presentation
5. The Finding of Jesus in the Temple

THE SORROWFUL MYSTERIES
(Tuesdays and Fridays, may be said on Sundays during Lent)

1. The Agony in the Garden
2. The Scourging at the Pillar
3. The Crowning with Thorns
4. The Carrying of the Cross
5. The Crucifixion

THE GLORIOUS MYSTERIES
(Wednesdays and Sundays)

1. The Resurrection
2. The Ascension
3. The Descent of the Holy Spirit
4. The Assumption of the Blessed Virgin Mary
5. The Coronation of the Blessed Virgin Mary

THE LUMINOUS MYSTERIES
(Thursdays)

1. The Baptism in the Jordan
2. The Wedding at Cana
3. Proclamation of the Kingdom
4. The Transfiguration
5. Institution of the Eucharist

Reflections: Mass, Homily & Scriptures

Date:

	Book	Chapter	Verses
1st Reading			
Responsorial			
2nd Reading			
Verse			
Gospel			

Notes

✠ Reflections ✠

Thank You Lord

Daily Reflections

My Jesus, I believe that You are present in the Most Holy Sacrament. I love You above all things, and I desire to receive You into my soul. Since I cannot at this moment receive You sacramentally, come at least spiritually into my heart. I embrace You as if You were already there and unite myself wholly to You. Never permit me to be separated from You. Amen.

Sunday		
Monday		
Tuesday		
Wednesday		
Thursday		
Friday		
Saturday		

The Spiritual Works of Mercy

To admonish sinners
To instruct the ignorant
To counsel the doubtful
To comfort the sorrowful
To bear wrongs patiently
To forgive all injuries
To pray for the living and the dead

I
T
r
u
s
t

J
e
s
u
s

The Corporal Works of Mercy

To feed the hungry
To give drink to the thirsty
To clothe the naked
To visit and ransom the captives
To shelter the homeless
To visit the sick
To bury the dead

Prayers & Answers

Date:	Date:
Prayer:	Prayer:
Answer:	Answer:

Daily Examination of Conscience

Sins:	Pride	Greed	Gluttony	Lust	Sloth	Envy	Anger
Virtues:	Humily	Generosity	Abstinence	Chastity	Diligence	Kindness	Patience

Sunday		
Monday		
Tuesday		
Wednesday		
Thursday		
Friday		
Saturday		

Act of Contrition

M
c
r
c
y

My God, I am sorry for my sins with all my heart. In
choosing to do wrong and failing to do good, I have
sinned against you whom I should love above all
things. I firmly intend, with your help, to do penance,
to sin no more, and to avoid whatever leads me to
sin. Our Savior Jesus Christ suffered and died for us.
In His name, my God, have mercy on us.

Forgiveness

Amen.

Prayers & Answers

Date:	Date:
Prayer:	Prayer:
Answer:	Answer:

Reflections: Mass, Homily & Scriptures

Date:

	Book	Chapter	Verses
1st Reading			
Responsorial			
2nd Reading			
Verse			
Gospel			

Notes

_____

_____

_____

_____

_____

_____

_____

_____

_____

_____

_____

_____

✠ Reflections ✠

_____

_____

_____

_____

_____

_____

_____

_____

_____

Thank You Lord

Daily Reflections

My Jesus, I believe that You are present in the Most Holy Sacrament. I love You above all things, and I desire to receive You into my soul. Since I cannot at this moment receive You sacramentally, come at least spiritually into my heart. I embrace You as if You were already there and unite myself wholly to You. Never permit me to be separated from You. Amen.

Sunday		
Monday		
Tuesday		
Wednesday		
Thursday		
Friday		
Saturday		

The Spiritual Works of Mercy

To admonish sinners
To instruct the ignorant
To counsel the doubtful
To comfort the sorrowful
To bear wrongs patiently
To forgive all injuries
To pray for the living and the dead

I
T
r
u
s
t

J
e
s
u
s

The Corporal Works of Mercy

To feed the hungry
To give drink to the thirsty
To clothe the naked
To visit and ransom the captives
To shelter the homeless
To visit the sick
To bury the dead

Prayers & Answers

Date:	Date:
Prayer:	Prayer:
Answer:	Answer:

Daily Examination of Conscience

Sins:	Pride	Greed	Gluttony	Lust	Sloth	Envy	Anger
Virtues:	Humily	Generosity	Abstinence	Chastity	Diligence	Kindness	Patience

Sunday		
Monday		
Tuesday		
Wednesday		
Thursday		
Friday		
Saturday		

Act of Contrition

M
e
r
c
y

My God, I am sorry for my sins with all my heart. In
choosing to do wrong and failing to do good, I have
sinned against you whom I should love above all
things. I firmly intend, with your help, to do penance,
to sin no more, and to avoid whatever leads me to
sin. Our Savior Jesus Christ suffered and died for us.
In His name, my God, have mercy on us.

F
o
r
g
i
v
e
n
e
s
s

Amen.

Prayers & Answers

Date:	Date:
Prayer:	Prayer:
Answer:	Answer:

Reflections: Mass, Homily & Scriptures

Date:

	Book	Chapter	Verses
1st Reading			
Responsorial			
2nd Reading			
Verse			
Gospel			

Notes

_____
_____
_____
_____
_____
_____
_____
_____
_____
_____
_____
_____
_____
_____

✠ Reflections ✠

_____
_____
_____
_____
_____
_____
_____
_____
_____
_____
_____
_____
_____
_____

Thank You Lord

Daily Reflections

My Jesus, I believe that You are present in the Most Holy Sacrament. I love You above all things, and I desire to receive You into my soul. Since I cannot at this moment receive You sacramentally, come at least spiritually into my heart. I embrace You as if You were already there and unite myself wholly to You. Never permit me to be separated from You. Amen.

Sunday		
Monday		
Tuesday		
Wednesday		
Thursday		
Friday		
Saturday		

The Spiritual Works of Mercy

To admonish sinners
To instruct the ignorant
To counsel the doubtful
To comfort the sorrowful
To bear wrongs patiently
To forgive all injuries
To pray for the living and the dead

I T r u s t

J e s u s

The Corporal Works of Mercy

To feed the hungry
To give drink to the thirsty
To clothe the naked
To visit and ransom the captives
To shelter the homeless
To visit the sick
To bury the dead

Prayers & Answers

Date:	Date:
Prayer:	Prayer:
Answer:	Answer:

Daily Examination of Conscience

Sins:	Pride	Greed	Gluttony	Lust	Sloth	Envy	Anger
Virtues:	Humily	Generosity	Abstinence	Chastity	Diligence	Kindness	Patience
Sunday							
Monday							
Tuesday							
Wednesday							
Thursday							
Friday							
Saturday							

Act of Contrition

M
e
r
c
y

My God, I am sorry for my sins with all my heart. In choosing to do wrong and failing to do good, I have sinned against you whom I should love above all things. I firmly intend, with your help, to do penance, to sin no more, and to avoid whatever leads me to sin. Our Savior Jesus Christ suffered and died for us. In His name, my God, have mercy on us.

Forgiveness

Amen.

Prayers & Answers

Date:	Date:
Prayer:	Prayer:
Answer:	Answer:

Reflections: Mass, Homily & Scriptures

Date:

	Book	Chapter	Verses
1st Reading			
Responsorial			
2nd Reading			
Verse			
Gospel			

Notes

✝ Reflections ✝

Thank You Lord

Daily Reflections

My Jesus, I believe that You are present in the Most Holy Sacrament. I love You above all things, and I desire to receive You into my soul. Since I cannot at this moment receive You sacramentally, come at least spiritually into my heart. I embrace You as if You were already there and unite myself wholly to You. Never permit me to be separated from You. Amen.

Sunday		
Monday		
Tuesday		
Wednesday		
Thursday		
Friday		
Saturday		

The Spiritual Works of Mercy

I
T
r
u
s
t

To admonish sinners
To instruct the ignorant
To counsel the doubtful
To comfort the sorrowful
To bear wrongs patiently
To forgive all injuries
To pray for the living and the dead

The Corporal Works of Mercy

J
e
s
u
s

To feed the hungry
To give drink to the thirsty
To clothe the naked
To visit and ransom the captives
To shelter the homeless
To visit the sick
To bury the dead

Prayers & Answers

Date:	Date:
Prayer:	Prayer:
Answer:	Answer:

Daily Examination of Conscience

Sins:	Pride	Greed	Gluttony	Lust	Sloth	Envy	Anger
Virtues:	Humily	Generosity	Abstinence	Chastity	Diligence	Kindness	Patience

Sunday		
Monday		
Tuesday		
Wednesday		
Thursday		
Friday		
Saturday		

Act of Contrition

M
c
r
c
y

My God, I am sorry for my sins with all my heart. In
choosing to do wrong and failing to do good, I have
sinned against you whom I should love above all
things. I firmly intend, with your help, to do penance,
to sin no more, and to avoid whatever leads me to
sin. Our Savior Jesus Christ suffered and died for us.
In His name, my God, have mercy on us.

F
o
r
g
i
v
e
n
e
s
s

Amen.

Prayers & Answers

Date:	Date:
Prayer:	Prayer:
Answer:	Answer:

Reflections: Mass, Homily & Scriptures

Date:

	Book	Chapter	Verses
1st Reading			
Responsorial			
2nd Reading			
Verse			
Gospel			

Notes

✞ Reflections ✞

Thank You Lord

Daily Reflections

My Jesus, I believe that You are present in the Most Holy Sacrament. I love You above all things, and I desire to receive You into my soul. Since I cannot at this moment receive You sacramentally, come at least spiritually into my heart. I embrace You as if You were already there and unite myself wholly to You. Never permit me to be separated from You. Amen.

Sunday		
Monday		
Tuesday		
Wednesday		
Thursday		
Friday		
Saturday		

The Spiritual Works of Mercy

To admonish sinners
To instruct the ignorant
To counsel the doubtful
To comfort the sorrowful
To bear wrongs patiently
To forgive all injuries
To pray for the living and the dead

I T r u s t

J e s u s

The Corporal Works of Mercy

To feed the hungry
To give drink to the thirsty
To clothe the naked
To visit and ransom the captives
To shelter the homeless
To visit the sick
To bury the dead

Prayers & Answers

Date:	Date:
Prayer:	Prayer:
Answer:	Answer:

Daily Examination of Conscience

Sins:	Pride	Greed	Gluttony	Lust	Sloth	Envy	Anger
Virtues:	Humily	Generosity	Abstinence	Chastity	Diligence	Kindness	Patience

Sunday		
Monday		
Tuesday		
Wednesday		
Thursday		
Friday		
Saturday		

Act of Contrition

M
e
r
c
y

My God, I am sorry for my sins with all my heart. In choosing to do wrong and failing to do good, I have sinned against you whom I should love above all things. I firmly intend, with your help, to do penance, to sin no more, and to avoid whatever leads me to sin. Our Savior Jesus Christ suffered and died for us. In His name, my God, have mercy on us.

F
o
r
g
i
v
e
n
e
s
s

Amen.

Prayers & Answers

Date:	Date:
Prayer:	Prayer:
Answer:	Answer:

On the day before He was to suffer…

...broke the bread and gave it to His disciples...

Stations of the Cross

1st Station: Jesus is condemned to death
2nd Station: Jesus carries His cross
3rd Station: Jesus falls the first time
4th Station: Jesus meets his mother
5th Station: Simon of Cyrene helps Jesus to carry his cross
6th Station: Veronica wipes the face of Jesus
7th Station: Jesus falls the second time
8th Station: Jesus meets the women of Jerusalem
9th Station: Jesus falls a third time
10th Station: Jesus clothes are taken away
11th Station: Jesus is nailed to the cross
12th Station: Jesus dies on the cross
13th Station: The body of Jesus is taken down from the cross
14th Station: Jesus is laid in the tomb

Reflections: Mass, Homily & Scriptures

Date:

	Book	Chapter	Verses
1st Reading			
Responsorial			
2nd Reading			
Verse			
Gospel			

Notes

✠ Reflections ✠

Thank You Lord

Daily Reflections

My Jesus, I believe that You are present in the Most Holy Sacrament. I love You above all things, and I desire to receive You into my soul. Since I cannot at this moment receive You sacramentally, come at least spiritually into my heart. I embrace You as if You were already there and unite myself wholly to You. Never permit me to be separated from You. Amen.

Sunday		
Monday		
Tuesday		
Wednesday		
Thursday		
Friday		
Saturday		

The Spiritual Works of Mercy

To admonish sinners
To instruct the ignorant
To counsel the doubtful
To comfort the sorrowful
To bear wrongs patiently
To forgive all injuries
To pray for the living and the dead

The Corporal Works of Mercy

To feed the hungry
To give drink to the thirsty
To clothe the naked
To visit and ransom the captives
To shelter the homeless
To visit the sick
To bury the dead

Prayers & Answers

Date:	Date:
Prayer:	Prayer:
Answer:	Answer:

Daily Examination of Conscience

SINS	Pride	Greed	Gluttony	Lust	Sloth	Envy	Anger
VIRTUES	Humility	Generosity	Abstinence	Chastity	Diligence	Kindness	Patience

Sunday		
Monday		
Tuesday		
Wednesday		
Thursday		
Friday		
Saturday		

M E R C Y

Act of Contrition

My God, I am sorry for my sins with all my heart.
In choosing to do wrong and failing to do good,
I have sinned against you whom I should love above all things.
I firmly intend, with your help, to do penance, to sin no more,
and to avoid whatever leads me to sin.
Our Savior Jesus Christ suffered and died for us.
In His name, my God, have mercy.
Amen.

F o r g i v e n e s s

Prayers & Answers

Date:	Date:
Prayer:	Prayer:
Answer:	Answer:
Date:	Date:
Prayer:	Prayer:
Answer:	Answer:

Reflections: Mass, Homily & Scriptures

Date:

	Book	Chapter	Verses
1st Reading			
Responsorial			
2nd Reading			
Verse			
Gospel			

Notes

✟ Reflections ✟

Thank You Lord

Daily Reflections

My Jesus, I believe that You are present in the Most Holy Sacrament. I love You above all things, and I desire to receive You into my soul. Since I cannot at this moment receive You sacramentally, come at least spiritually into my heart. I embrace You as if You were already there and unite myself wholly to You. Never permit me to be separated from You. Amen.

Sunday		
Monday		
Tuesday		
Wednesday		
Thursday		
Friday		
Saturday		

The Spiritual Works of Mercy

To admonish sinners

To instruct the ignorant

To counsel the doubtful

To comfort the sorrowful

To bear wrongs patiently

To forgive all injuries

To pray for the living and the dead

The Corporal Works of Mercy

To feed the hungry

To give drink to the thirsty

To clothe the naked

To visit and ransom the captives

To shelter the homeless

To visit the sick

To bury the dead

Prayers & Answers

Date:	Date:
Prayer:	Prayer:
Answer:	Answer:

Daily Examination of Conscience

SINS	Pride	Greed	Gluttony	Lust	Sloth	Envy	Anger
VIRTUES	Humility	Generosity	Abstinence	Chastity	Diligence	Kindness	Patience

Sunday		
Monday		
Tuesday		
Wednesday		
Thursday		
Friday		
Saturday		

M
E
R
C
Y

Act of Contrition

My God, I am sorry for my sins with all my heart.
In choosing to do wrong and failing to do good,
I have sinned against you whom I should love above all things.
I firmly intend, with your help, to do penance, to sin no more,
and to avoid whatever leads me to sin.
Our Savior Jesus Christ suffered and died for us.
In His name, my God, have mercy.
Amen.

F
o
r
g
i
v
e
n
e
s
s

Prayers & Answers

Date:

Prayer:

Answer:

Date:

Prayer:

Answer:

Date:

Prayer:

Answer:

Date:

Prayer:

Answer:

Reflections: Mass, Homily & Scriptures

Date:

	Book	Chapter	Verses
1st Reading			
Responsorial			
2nd Reading			
Verse			
Gospel			

Notes

_____
_____
_____
_____
_____
_____
_____
_____
_____
_____
_____
_____
_____
_____

✝ Reflections ✝

_____
_____
_____
_____
_____
_____
_____
_____
_____
_____
_____
_____

Thank You Lord

Daily Reflections

My Jesus, I believe that You are present in the Most Holy Sacrament. I love You above all things, and I desire to receive You into my soul. Since I cannot at this moment receive You sacramentally, come at least spiritually into my heart. I embrace You as if You were already there and unite myself wholly to You. Never permit me to be separated from You. Amen.

Sunday		
Monday		
Tuesday		
Wednesday		
Thursday		
Friday		
Saturday		

The Spiritual Works of Mercy

To admonish sinners

To instruct the ignorant

To counsel the doubtful

To comfort the sorrowful

To bear wrongs patiently

To forgive all injuries

To pray for the living and the dead

The Corporal Works of Mercy

To feed the hungry

To give drink to the thirsty

To clothe the naked

To visit and ransom the captives

To shelter the homeless

To visit the sick

To bury the dead

Prayers & Answers

Date:	Date:
Prayer:	Prayer:
Answer:	Answer:

Daily Examination of Conscience

Sins:	Pride	Greed	Gluttony	Lust	Sloth	Envy	Anger
Virtues:	Humily	Generosity	Abstinence	Chastity	Diligence	Kindness	Patience

Sunday		
Monday		
Tuesday		
Wednesday		
Thursday		
Friday		
Saturday		

Act of Contrition

M
e
r
c
y

My God, I am sorry for my sins with all my heart. In
choosing to do wrong and failing to do good, I have
sinned against you whom I should love above all
things. I firmly intend, with your help, to do penance,
to sin no more, and to avoid whatever leads me to
sin. Our Savior Jesus Christ suffered and died for us.
In His name, my God, have mercy on us.

Forgiveness

Amen.

Prayers & Answers

Date:		Date:	
Prayer:		Prayer:	
Answer:		Answer:	

Reflections: Mass, Homily & Scriptures

Date:

	Book	Chapter	Verses
1st Reading			
Responsorial			
2nd Reading			
Verse			
Gospel			

Notes

✠ Reflections ✠

Thank You Lord

Daily Reflections

My Jesus, I believe that You are present in the Most Holy Sacrament. I love You above all things, and I desire to receive You into my soul. Since I cannot at this moment receive You sacramentally, come at least spiritually into my heart. I embrace You as if You were already there and unite myself wholly to You. Never permit me to be separated from You. Amen.

Sunday		
Monday		
Tuesday		
Wednesday		
Thursday		
Friday		
Saturday		

The Spiritual Works of Mercy

To admonish sinners
To instruct the ignorant
To counsel the doubtful
To comfort the sorrowful
To bear wrongs patiently
To forgive all injuries
To pray for the living and the dead

I
T
r
u
s
t

J
e
s
u
s

The Corporal Works of Mercy

To feed the hungry
To give drink to the thirsty
To clothe the naked
To visit and ransom the captives
To shelter the homeless
To visit the sick
To bury the dead

Prayers & Answers

Date:	Date:
Prayer:	Prayer:
Answer:	Answer:

Daily Examination of Conscience

Sins:	Pride	Greed	Gluttony	Lust	Sloth	Envy	Anger
Virtues:	Humily	Generosity	Abstinence	Chastity	Diligence	Kindness	Patience

Sunday		
Monday		
Tuesday		
Wednesday		
Thursday		
Friday		
Saturday		

Act of Contrition

M
e
r
c
y

My God, I am sorry for my sins with all my heart. In choosing to do wrong and failing to do good, I have sinned against you whom I should love above all things. I firmly intend, with your help, to do penance, to sin no more, and to avoid whatever leads me to sin. Our Savior Jesus Christ suffered and died for us. In His name, my God, have mercy on us.

F
o
r
g
i
v
e
n
e
s
s

Amen.

Prayers & Answers

Date:	Date:
Prayer:	Prayer:
Answer:	Answer:

Reflections: Mass, Homily & Scriptures

Date:

	Book	Chapter	Verses
1st Reading			
Responsorial			
2nd Reading			
Verse			
Gospel			

Notes

✟ Reflections ✟

Thank You Lord

Daily Reflections

My Jesus, I believe that You are present in the Most Holy Sacrament. I love You above all things, and I desire to receive You into my soul. Since I cannot at this moment receive You sacramentally, come at least spiritually into my heart. I embrace You as if You were already there and unite myself wholly to You. Never permit me to be separated from You. Amen.

Sunday		
Monday		
Tuesday		
Wednesday		
Thursday		
Friday		
Saturday		

The Spiritual Works of Mercy	I T r u s t	The Corporal Works of Mercy
To admonish sinners		To feed the hungry
To instruct the ignorant	J e s u s	To give drink to the thirsty
To counsel the doubtful		To clothe the naked
To comfort the sorrowful		To visit and ransom the captives
To bear wrongs patiently		To shelter the homeless
To forgive all injuries		To visit the sick
To pray for the living and the dead		To bury the dead

Prayers & Answers

Date:	Date:
Prayer:	Prayer:
Answer:	Answer:

Daily Examination of Conscience

Sins:	Pride	Greed	Gluttony	Lust	Sloth	Envy	Anger
Virtues:	Humily	Generosity	Abstinence	Chastity	Diligence	Kindness	Patience

Sunday		
Monday		
Tuesday		
Wednesday		
Thursday		
Friday		
Saturday		

Act of Contrition

M
e
r
c
y

My God, I am sorry for my sins with all my heart. In
choosing to do wrong and failing to do good, I have
sinned against you whom I should love above all
things. I firmly intend, with your help, to do penance,
to sin no more, and to avoid whatever leads me to
sin. Our Savior Jesus Christ suffered and died for us.
In His name, my God, have mercy on us.

F
o
r
g
i
v
e
n
e
s
s

Amen.

Prayers & Answers

Date:	Date:
Prayer:	Prayer:
Answer:	Answer:

By your cross and
resurrection…

Of the new and eternal
covenant…

St. Michael the Archangel Prayer

*St. Michael the Archangel,
defend us in battle.*

*Be our defense against the wickedness and snares
of the Devil.*

*May God rebuke him, we humbly pray,
and do thou,
O Prince of the heavenly hosts,
by the power of God,
thrust into hell Satan,
and all the evil spirits,
who prowl about the world
seeking the ruin of souls.*

Amen.

Reflections: Mass, Homily & Scriptures

Date:

	Book	Chapter	Verses
1st Reading			
Responsorial			
2nd Reading			
Verse			
Gospel			

Notes

✠ Reflections ✠

Thank You Lord

Daily Reflections

My Jesus, I believe that You are present in the Most Holy Sacrament. I love You above all things, and I desire to receive You into my soul. Since I cannot at this moment receive You sacramentally, come at least spiritually into my heart. I embrace You as if You were already there and unite myself wholly to You. Never permit me to be separated from You. Amen.

Sunday		
Monday		
Tuesday		
Wednesday		
Thursday		
Friday		
Saturday		

The Spiritual Works of Mercy

To admonish sinners
To instruct the ignorant
To counsel the doubtful
To comfort the sorrowful
To bear wrongs patiently
To forgive all injuries
To pray for the living and the dead

I T r u s t

J e s u s

The Corporal Works of Mercy

To feed the hungry
To give drink to the thirsty
To clothe the naked
To visit and ransom the captives
To shelter the homeless
To visit the sick
To bury the dead

Prayers & Answers

Date:	Date:
Prayer:	Prayer:
Answer:	Answer:

Daily Examination of Conscience

Sins:	Pride	Greed	Gluttony	Lust	Sloth	Envy	Anger
Virtues:	Humily	Generosity	Abstinence	Chastity	Diligence	Kindness	Patience

Sunday			
Monday			
Tuesday			
Wednesday			
Thursday			
Friday			
Saturday			

Act of Contrition

M
e
r
c
y

My God, I am sorry for my sins with all my heart. In
choosing to do wrong and failing to do good, I have
sinned against you whom I should love above all
things. I firmly intend, with your help, to do penance,
to sin no more, and to avoid whatever leads me to
sin. Our Savior Jesus Christ suffered and died for us.
In His name, my God, have mercy on us.
                                                            Amen.

F
o
r
g
i
v
e
n
e
s
s

Prayers & Answers

Date:	Date:
Prayer:	Prayer:
Answer:	Answer:

Reflections: Mass, Homily & Scriptures

Date:

	Book	Chapter	Verses
1st Reading			
Responsorial			
2nd Reading			
Verse			
Gospel			

Notes

✝ Reflections ✝

Thank You Lord

Daily Reflections

My Jesus, I believe that You are present in the Most Holy Sacrament. I love You above all things, and I desire to receive You into my soul. Since I cannot at this moment receive You sacramentally, come at least spiritually into my heart. I embrace You as if You were already there and unite myself wholly to You. Never permit me to be separated from You. Amen.

Sunday		
Monday		
Tuesday		
Wednesday		
Thursday		
Friday		
Saturday		

The Spiritual Works of Mercy

To admonish sinners
To instruct the ignorant
To counsel the doubtful
To comfort the sorrowful
To bear wrongs patiently
To forgive all injuries
To pray for the living and the dead

Illustrous Jesus

The Corporal Works of Mercy

To feed the hungry
To give drink to the thirsty
To clothe the naked
To visit and ransom the captives
To shelter the homeless
To visit the sick
To bury the dead

Prayers & Answers

Date:	Date:
Prayer:	Prayer:
Answer:	Answer:

Daily Examination of Conscience

Sins:	Pride	Greed	Gluttony	Lust	Sloth	Envy	Anger
Virtues:	Humily	Generosity	Abstinence	Chastity	Diligence	Kindness	Patience

Sunday		
Monday		
Tuesday		
Wednesday		
Thursday		
Friday		
Saturday		

Act of Contrition

M
e
r
c
y

My God, I am sorry for my sins with all my heart. In
choosing to do wrong and failing to do good, I have
sinned against you whom I should love above all
things. I firmly intend, with your help, to do penance,
to sin no more, and to avoid whatever leads me to
sin. Our Savior Jesus Christ suffered and died for us.
In His name, my God, have mercy on us.

Forgiveness

Amen.

Prayers & Answers

Date:	Date:
Prayer:	Prayer:
Answer:	Answer:

Reflections: Mass, Homily & Scriptures

Date:

	Book	Chapter	Verses
1st Reading			
Responsorial			
2nd Reading			
Verse			
Gospel			

Notes

✠ Reflections ✠

Thank You Lord

Daily Reflections

My Jesus, I believe that You are present in the Most Holy Sacrament. I love You above all things, and I desire to receive You into my soul. Since I cannot at this moment receive You sacramentally, come at least spiritually into my heart. I embrace You as if You were already there and unite myself wholly to You. Never permit me to be separated from You. Amen.

Sunday		
Monday		
Tuesday		
Wednesday		
Thursday		
Friday		
Saturday		

The Spiritual Works of Mercy

To admonish sinners

To instruct the ignorant

To counsel the doubtful

To comfort the sorrowful

To bear wrongs patiently

To forgive all injuries

To pray for the living and the dead

I
T
r
u
s
t

J
e
s
u
s

The Corporal Works of Mercy

To feed the hungry

To give drink to the thirsty

To clothe the naked

To visit and ransom the captives

To shelter the homeless

To visit the sick

To bury the dead

Prayers & Answers

Date:	Date:
Prayer:	Prayer:
Answer:	Answer:

Daily Examination of Conscience

Sins:	Pride	Greed	Gluttony	Lust	Sloth	Envy	Anger
Virtues:	Humily	Generosity	Abstinence	Chastity	Diligence	Kindness	Patience

Sunday		
Monday		
Tuesday		
Wednesday		
Thursday		
Friday		
Saturday		

Act of Contrition

M
e
r
c
y

My God, I am sorry for my sins with all my heart. In
choosing to do wrong and failing to do good, I have
sinned against you whom I should love above all
things. I firmly intend, with your help, to do penance,
to sin no more, and to avoid whatever leads me to
sin. Our Savior Jesus Christ suffered and died for us.
In His name, my God, have mercy on us.

F
o
r
g
i
v
e
n
e
s
s

Amen.

Prayers & Answers

Date:	Date:
Prayer:	Prayer:
Answer:	Answer:

Reflections: Mass, Homily & Scriptures

Date:

	Book	Chapter	Verses
1st Reading			
Responsorial			
2nd Reading			
Verse			
Gospel			

Notes

_____
_____
_____
_____
_____
_____
_____
_____
_____
_____
_____
_____

✠ Reflections ✠

_____
_____
_____
_____
_____
_____
_____
_____
_____
_____

Thank You Lord

Daily Reflections

My Jesus, I believe that You are present in the Most Holy Sacrament. I love You above all things, and I desire to receive You into my soul. Since I cannot at this moment receive You sacramentally, come at least spiritually into my heart. I embrace You as if You were already there and unite myself wholly to You. Never permit me to be separated from You. Amen.

Sunday		
Monday		
Tuesday		
Wednesday		
Thursday		
Friday		
Saturday		

The Spiritual Works of Mercy

To admonish sinners
To instruct the ignorant
To counsel the doubtful
To comfort the sorrowful
To bear wrongs patiently
To forgive all injuries
To pray for the living and the dead

I T r u s t

J e s u s

The Corporal Works of Mercy

To feed the hungry
To give drink to the thirsty
To clothe the naked
To visit and ransom the captives
To shelter the homeless
To visit the sick
To bury the dead

Prayers & Answers

Date:	Date:
Prayer:	Prayer:
Answer:	Answer:

Daily Examination of Conscience

Sins:	Pride	Greed	Gluttony	Lust	Sloth	Envy	Anger
Virtues:	Humily	Generosity	Abstinence	Chastity	Diligence	Kindness	Patience

Sunday		
Monday		
Tuesday		
Wednesday		
Thursday		
Friday		
Saturday		

Act of Contrition

M
e
r
c
y

My God, I am sorry for my sins with all my heart. In
choosing to do wrong and failing to do good, I have
sinned against you whom I should love above all
things. I firmly intend, with your help, to do penance,
to sin no more, and to avoid whatever leads me to
sin. Our Savior Jesus Christ suffered and died for us.
In His name, my God, have mercy on us.

F
o
r
g
i
v
e
n
e
s
s

Amen.

Prayers & Answers

Date:	Date:
Prayer:	Prayer:
Answer:	Answer:

Reflections: Mass, Homily & Scriptures

Date:

	Book	Chapter	Verses
1st Reading			
Responsorial			
2nd Reading			
Verse			
Gospel			

Notes

☦ Reflections ☦

Thank You Lord

Daily Reflections

My Jesus, I believe that You are present in the Most Holy Sacrament. I love You above all things, and I desire to receive You into my soul. Since I cannot at this moment receive You sacramentally, come at least spiritually into my heart. I embrace You as if You were already there and unite myself wholly to You. Never permit me to be separated from You. Amen.

Sunday		
Monday		
Tuesday		
Wednesday		
Thursday		
Friday		
Saturday		

The Spiritual Works of Mercy

To admonish sinners
To instruct the ignorant
To counsel the doubtful
To comfort the sorrowful
To bear wrongs patiently
To forgive all injuries
To pray for the living and the dead

Trust Jesus

The Corporal Works of Mercy

To feed the hungry
To give drink to the thirsty
To clothe the naked
To visit and ransom the captives
To shelter the homeless
To visit the sick
To bury the dead

Prayers & Answers

Date:	Date:
Prayer:	Prayer:
Answer:	Answer:

Daily Examination of Conscience

Sins:	Pride	Greed	Gluttony	Lust	Sloth	Envy	Anger
Virtues:	Humily	Generosity	Abstinence	Chastity	Diligence	Kindness	Patience

Sunday		
Monday		
Tuesday		
Wednesday		
Thursday		
Friday		
Saturday		

Act of Contrition

M
e
r
c
y

My God, I am sorry for my sins with all my heart. In
choosing to do wrong and failing to do good, I have
sinned against you whom I should love above all
things. I firmly intend, with your help, to do penance,
to sin no more, and to avoid whatever leads me to
sin. Our Savior Jesus Christ suffered and died for us.
In His name, my God, have mercy on us.

F
o
r
g
i
v
e
n
e
s
s

Amen.

Prayers & Answers

Date:		Date:	
Prayer:		Prayer:	
Answer:		Answer:	

Live no longer for
ourselves but for Him who
died for us…

Alleluia!

Glory Be

Glory be to the Father,
and to the Son,
and to the Holy Spirit.
As it was in the beginning,
is now,
and ever shall be,
world without end.

Amen.

Reflections: Mass, Homily & Scriptures

Date:

	Book	Chapter	Verses
1st Reading			
Responsorial			
2nd Reading			
Verse			
Gospel			

Notes

_____
_____
_____
_____
_____
_____
_____
_____
_____
_____
_____
_____
_____

✝ Reflections ✝

_____
_____
_____
_____
_____
_____
_____
_____
_____
_____
_____
_____

Thank You Lord

Daily Reflections

My Jesus, I believe that You are present in the Most Holy Sacrament. I love You above all things, and I desire to receive You into my soul. Since I cannot at this moment receive You sacramentally, come at least spiritually into my heart. I embrace You as if You were already there and unite myself wholly to You. Never permit me to be separated from You. Amen.

Sunday		
Monday		
Tuesday		
Wednesday		
Thursday		
Friday		
Saturday		

The Spiritual Works of Mercy

I
T
r
u
s
t

J
e
s
u
s

To admonish sinners
To instruct the ignorant
To counsel the doubtful
To comfort the sorrowful
To bear wrongs patiently
To forgive all injuries
To pray for the living and the dead

The Corporal Works of Mercy

To feed the hungry
To give drink to the thirsty
To clothe the naked
To visit and ransom the captives
To shelter the homeless
To visit the sick
To bury the dead

Prayers & Answers

Date:	Date:
Prayer:	Prayer:
Answer:	Answer:

Daily Examination of Conscience

Sins:	Pride	Greed	Gluttony	Lust	Sloth	Envy	Anger
Virtues:	Humiliy	Generosity	Abstinence	Chastity	Diligence	Kindness	Patience

Sunday		
Monday		
Tuesday		
Wednesday		
Thursday		
Friday		
Saturday		

Act of Contrition

M
e
r
c
y

My God, I am sorry for my sins with all my heart. In choosing to do wrong and failing to do good, I have sinned against you whom I should love above all things. I firmly intend, with your help, to do penance, to sin no more, and to avoid whatever leads me to sin. Our Savior Jesus Christ suffered and died for us. In His name, my God, have mercy on us.

F
o
r
g
i
v
e
n
e
s
s

Amen.

Prayers & Answers

Date:	Date:
Prayer:	Prayer:
Answer:	Answer:

Reflections: Mass, Homily & Scriptures

Date:

	Book	Chapter	Verses
1st Reading			
Responsorial			
2nd Reading			
Verse			
Gospel			

Notes

✠ Reflections ✠

Thank You Lord

Daily Reflections

My Jesus, I believe that You are present in the Most Holy Sacrament. I love You above all things, and I desire to receive You into my soul. Since I cannot at this moment receive You sacramentally, come at least spiritually into my heart. I embrace You as if You were already there and unite myself wholly to You. Never permit me to be separated from You. Amen.

Sunday		
Monday		
Tuesday		
Wednesday		
Thursday		
Friday		
Saturday		

The Spiritual Works of Mercy

To admonish sinners
To instruct the ignorant
To counsel the doubtful
To comfort the sorrowful
To bear wrongs patiently
To forgive all injuries
To pray for the living and the dead

I
T
r
u
s
t

J
e
s
u
s

The Corporal Works of Mercy

To feed the hungry
To give drink to the thirsty
To clothe the naked
To visit and ransom the captives
To shelter the homeless
To visit the sick
To bury the dead

Prayers & Answers

Date:	Date:
Prayer:	Prayer:
Answer:	Answer:

Daily Examination of Conscience

Sins:	Pride	Greed	Gluttony	Lust	Sloth	Envy	Anger
Virtues:	Humily	Generosity	Abstinence	Chastity	Diligence	Kindness	Patience

Sunday		
Monday		
Tuesday		
Wednesday		
Thursday		
Friday		
Saturday		

Act of Contrition

M
c
r
c
y

My God, I am sorry for my sins with all my heart. In choosing to do wrong and failing to do good, I have sinned against you whom I should love above all things. I firmly intend, with your help, to do penance, to sin no more, and to avoid whatever leads me to sin. Our Savior Jesus Christ suffered and died for us. In His name, my God, have mercy on us.

Forgiveness

Amen.

Prayers & Answers

Date:	Date:
Prayer:	Prayer:
Answer:	Answer:

Reflections: Mass, Homily & Scriptures

Date:

	Book	Chapter	Verses
1st Reading			
Responsorial			
2nd Reading			
Verse			
Gospel			

Notes

✚ Reflections ✚

Thank You Lord

Daily Reflections

My Jesus, I believe that You are present in the Most Holy Sacrament. I love You above all things, and I desire to receive You into my soul. Since I cannot at this moment receive You sacramentally, come at least spiritually into my heart. I embrace You as if You were already there and unite myself wholly to You. Never permit me to be separated from You. Amen.

Sunday		
Monday		
Tuesday		
Wednesday		
Thursday		
Friday		
Saturday		

The Spiritual Works of Mercy

To admonish sinners

To instruct the ignorant

To counsel the doubtful

To comfort the sorrowful

To bear wrongs patiently

To forgive all injuries

To pray for the living and the dead

The Corporal Works of Mercy

To feed the hungry

To give drink to the thirsty

To clothe the naked

To visit and ransom the captives

To shelter the homeless

To visit the sick

To bury the dead

Prayers & Answers

Date:	Date:
Prayer:	Prayer:
Answer:	Answer:

Daily Examination of Conscience

Sins:	Pride	Greed	Gluttony	Lust	Sloth	Envy	Anger
Virtues:	Humily	Generosity	Abstinence	Chastity	Diligence	Kindness	Patience

Sunday		
Monday		
Tuesday		
Wednesday		
Thursday		
Friday		
Saturday		

Act of Contrition

M
e
r
c
y

My God, I am sorry for my sins with all my heart. In choosing to do wrong and failing to do good, I have sinned against you whom I should love above all things. I firmly intend, with your help, to do penance, to sin no more, and to avoid whatever leads me to sin. Our Savior Jesus Christ suffered and died for us. In His name, my God, have mercy on us.

F
o
r
g
i
v
e
n
e
s
s

Amen.

Prayers & Answers

Date:	Date:
Prayer:	Prayer:
Answer:	Answer:

Pray Always

Date:

Prayer:

Answer:

Date:

Prayer:

Answer:

Date:

Prayer:

Answer:

Date:

Prayer:

Answer:

Date:

Prayer:

Answer:

Date:

Prayer:

Answer:

Date:

Prayer:

Answer:

Pray Always

Date:

Prayer:

Answer:

Date:

Prayer:

Answer:

Date:

Prayer:

Answer:

Date:

Prayer:

Answer:

Date:

Prayer:

Answer:

Date:

Prayer:

Answer:

Date:

Prayer:

Answer:

Pray Always

Date:

Prayer:

Answer:

Date:

Prayer:

Answer:

Date:

Prayer:

Answer:

Date:

Prayer:

Answer:

Date:

Prayer:

Answer:

Date:

Prayer:

Answer:

Date:

Prayer:

Answer:

Pray Always

Date:

Prayer:

Answer:

Date:

Prayer:

Answer:

Date:

Prayer:

Answer:

Date:

Prayer:

Answer:

Date:

Prayer:

Answer:

Date:

Prayer:

Answer:

Date:

Prayer:

Answer:

Pray Always

Date:

Prayer:

Answer:

Date:

Prayer:

Answer:

Date:

Prayer:

Answer:

Date:

Prayer:

Answer:

Date:

Prayer:

Answer:

Date:

Prayer:

Answer:

Date:

Prayer:

Answer:

Pray Always

Date:

Prayer:

Answer:

Date:

Prayer:

Answer:

Date:

Prayer:

Answer:

Date:

Prayer:

Answer:

Date:

Prayer:

Answer:

Date:

Prayer:

Answer:

Date:

Prayer:

Answer:

Go in Peace!

Thanks be to God!

Prayer after Mass

Lord Jesus Christ, take all my freedom,
my memory, my understanding, and my will.
All that I have and cherish
you have given me.
I surrender it all to be guided by Your will.
Your grace and Your love
are enough for me.
Give me these, Lord Jesus,
and I ask for nothing more.

Amen.

"Lord look upon me with the eyes of your mercy. May your healing hand rest upon me. May your life giving power flow into every cell of my body + into the depths of my soul cleansing, purifying + restoring me to the wholeness + strength for service in your Kingdom. For God you are the only source of health + healing. The spirit of calm + central peace in the Universe. Grant me such a consciousness of your indwelling + surrounding presence that I may permit you to give me health + strength + peace through Jesus Christ our Lord." Amen

Holy Spirit may my heart be open to the work of God. May my heart be open to the good of God. May my heart be open to the beauty of God everyday. Lord do with you will with me in me + through me. Christ be before me, behind me, above me, below me + all around me + within me. Amen

Made in the USA
Middletown, DE
30 October 2018